MW01484977

Reiki:
The Comprehensive Guide

*How to Increase Energy, Improve Health,
and Feel Amazing with Reiki Healing*

Third Edition

**By
Jason Williams**

Table Of Contents

Introduction

I want to thank you and congratulate you for purchasing the book, *"Reiki: The Comprehensive Guide – How to Increase Energy, Improve Health, and Feel Amazing with Reiki Healing."*

This book contains proven steps and strategies on how to apply Reiki healing to have a happier, healthier, and better life.

As people seek for effective healing techniques that can improve their lives and set them free from stress and illnesses, the Reiki system of natural healing has become popular across the globe. Many people who have tried the Reiki healing claimed to have experienced amazing and healing effects in their body, mind, and spirit.

The term *Reiki* corresponds to the Universal Life Force Energy that is present within and around all living and nonliving entities. The term *Rei* denotes the Universal Divine Spirit and the term *Ki* denotes the life energy. It is said that the life energy in Reiki healing is comparable to the "light" in Christianity, "Chi" in acupuncture, and "Prana" in Yogic traditions.

The Reiki system of natural healing was founded by Dr. Mikao Usui, a Japanese Buddhist practitioner with an extensive knowledge in various religious teachings and philosophies. While Usui's Reiki system may involve a type of spiritual practice that is compatible with traditional and modern medical treatments and methods, Reiki is not considered a religion. It does not have anything to do with any specific religious belief or doctrine. Thus, everyone can participate and practice in sessions of the Reiki system of natural healing regardless of faith, religion, gender, age, race, or educational attainment. Anyone can take part in Reiki healing sessions in spite of his or her religious principles.

The Reiki system of natural healing encompasses different techniques that allow the subtle energy to flow through the hands of an individual into the subtle energy system. Reiki healing restores one's energy and vitality through relieving both emotional and physical effects of subdued tension and stress. While Reiki healing may appear to be extremely powerful, it is gentle and efficient in terms of nourishing an individual's body, mind, and spirit and opening blocked chakras.

The most significant purpose of Reiki healing is to bring the highest good or the subtle energy to an individual during a treatment session, particularly in the areas where healing is most needed. In addition, Reiki healing can also alleviate one's emotions along with the mind, body, and spirit through relaxation and revitalization.

Reiki healing can help in detoxifying one's body. It can also help in the fast treatment and recovery process of various types of diseases and illnesses. At the same time, Reiki healing can aid in releasing blockages in one's energy field through awakening his healing ability. During a Reiki healing session, creativity can be enhanced, relationships can be healed, and goals can be manifested.

The manner in which the Reiki system of natural healing is taught is distinct from other healing techniques. A Reiki master channels or transfers the Reiki life energy to the student during the process of attunement, wherein the crown, the heart, and the palm chakras are opened. These parts of the body are considered as the energy centers. Furthermore, during the process of attunement, the Reiki master, the student, and the Spirit or energy source establishes an extraordinary bond between them.

In the process of attunement, the student goes through an effective spiritual experience in which the energies are transferred through the laying of the Reiki master's hands and breathing on the crown chakra. As the energies are transferred, the student increases his psychic awareness and sensitivity. At the same time, the student also obtains the subtle energy and keeps it for a lifetime.

During a session of the Reiki system of natural healing, the client will be asked to lay on a massage table with clothes on. The Reiki practitioner or the one who will conduct the healing will discern the aura or body part that needs healing. Once the aura or body part is discerned, the practitioner will place his or her hands above the client's body. The practitioner will then run his or her hands slowly from the client's head to feet. A standard protocol for hand positions will be followed. On the other hand, some Reiki practitioner who is already adept with the Reiki healing follows their own intuition to treat themselves or other people. In general, a Reiki healing session will last for an hour or two. At the end of the session, an aura cleansing method will be carried out. The client will be asked to increase his or her fluid intake in order to release toxins and relax the body. In addition, the client will also be instructed to conduct his or her own healing meditation and affirmation.

An individual who receives the Reiki life energy is able to open his or her mind and heart towards his or her True Self. This is because the path of Reiki is one that endures a lifetime for one's personal and spiritual growth. Thus, an individual who obtains the life energy of the Reiki system of natural healing will not only become a student throughout his life, but will also continue to discover that what he truly needs lies within him.

In Chapter 1 of this book, you will learn what Reiki healing is as well as its principles and concepts. In this chapter, you will also learn how to become a Reiki practitioner. In Chapter 2, you will learn about the Reiki symbols, which include the *Cho Ku Rei* (power symbol), *Sei He* Ki (mental and emotional symbol), and the *Hon Sha Ze Sho Nen* (distance symbol). This chapter also discusses the purposes of these symbols and how to use them. Chapter 3 will discuss the uncommon uses of the Reiki symbols that you would not think possible. Chapter 4 presents a detailed discussion about the Reiki Master Level, which includes the Master attunement. In this chapter, you will learn the characteristics of Reiki Masters and practitioners in terms of professional conduct, professional appearance, professional excellence, professional integrity, health history/referrals, intention and reliance, communication and privacy, equality, awareness, student rights, and respect of cliencts. Furthermore, this chapter will discuss about the Reiki Master symbol, its uses, how it works, and how it can be integrated with the other Reiki symbols. You will also learn how Reiki Masters prefer their students to prepare for an attunement as well as how the Masters give their attunements in three parts. In Chapter 5, you will learn about the benefits of Reiki healing for your body, mind, and spirit. Chapter 6 discusses how Reiki healing works. It also discusses the significance of an exchange of energy based on the experience of Dr. Mikao Usui at the Beggar's Quarters in Kyoto. In

Chapter 7, you will learn about Reiki and its relationship with the main chakras. Chapter 8 provides information about the different Reiki hand positions for treating one's self and others. In Chapter 9 of this book, you will learn how Reiki healing can bring about positive changes in different aspects of your life. Chapter 10 discusses about how you can use the Reiki for emotional healing. Finally, Chapter 11 discusses how Reiki can heal even at a distance.

Thanks again for purchasing this book, I hope you enjoy it!

CHAPTER 1

What is Reiki Healing?

Background

The development of the Reiki system of natural healing and how it sustained its significance could be understood better by having a little knowledge about its founder, Mikao Usui.

Mikao Usui, who was born on August 15, 1865 in the village of Miyama-cho, formerly Taniai-mura, belonged from the high Samurai ranks of "Hatamoto." Usui's family was also followers of the Tendai Buddhist.

Japan started opening its doors to the outside world three years after Usui's birth. This unfolding brought an outburst of new ideas such as a radical change in Japan's educational system into European models. Thereafter, Japan embraced the concept of "westernization." However, after some time, people began reviving their feelings of conservatism and nationalism with emphasis on the principles of Confucianism and Shinto.

Meanwhile, as Japan continued to search for its development in the fields of arts and sciences, native Japanese movements gained their popularity. For instance, there was improvement in the martial arts of Jujitsu and Aiki Jutsu and various forms of Japanese self-defense arts such as Aikido were established. These new forms of martial arts were based on spiritual beliefs and values. In addition, palm healing methods also surfaced during this time.

The period of Japan's "westernization" brought about the development of new spiritual systems and healing techniques. When Usui was four years old, his parents sent him to a monastery of the Tendai Buddhist. It was in this monastery that Usui's curiosity in spiritual healing methods was awakened. Consequently, Usui became an enormously spiritual individual who chose to follow the Buddhist teachings.

When Usui was twelve years old, he started practicing the martial art of Aiki Jutsu, which was grounded in spiritual values. In his mid-twenties, Usui attained the highest level of Menkyo Kaiden as well as the highest levels of other traditional Japanese techniques.

As a student, Usui was said to be industrious, spending most of his free time reading books, particularly about theology, medicine, psychology, and fortune telling. His curiosity and persistence made him gain vast knowledge on different fields. He spent a great deal of time at the library of Kyoto University researching about his interests. This library kept sacred texts from various countries across the globe.

As a young man, Usui worked as a bodyguard or a diplomatic aide in which he had the opportunity to travel to different parts of the world including Europe, America, and China.

There was a point in Usui's life when he wondered about his purpose in life; thus, he sought for the answer. As he was trying to understand and seek a response to his pursuit, he received an enlightenment that revealed the ultimate purpose in life. Usui found out that this purpose was to have a completely peaceful state of mind and being aware of what to do with life without distractions. This is known as the *Anshin Rytsu Mei*. It took Usui three years to obtain the ultimate purpose in life.

Usui then decided to perform a 21-day fasting and meditation based on the teachings of the Tendai Buddhist. He went to Mt. Kurama and carried out the "Lotus Repentance Meditation." In the end, Usui received enlightenment or a "satori," which led him to establish his healing system.

Usui's healing system was grounded on the esoteric principles, traditional Chinese medicine methods, energy-transfer techniques such as Chi Kung, and martial arts. He integrated all these influences to come up with an efficient healing system, now known as the Reiki system of healing.

Usui made use of symbols in his healing system, which makes it obvious that it was grounded on mystical Shintoism. The use of energy exercises and traditional empowerments in Usui's healing system was based on Tendai Buddhism. Usui used a technique that allowed an individual to permanently bond with a healing source of energy.

Primarily, Usui's Reiki system of healing was based on obtaining personal rewards as soon as one understands and accepts his ultimate purpose and life. The Reiki system was also based on gaining contentment and achieving enlightenment.

On the other hand, the healing benefits of the Reiki system were originally just an added factor. The healing part of the Reiki system was referred to as *Teaté* or hand healing or application. As mentioned earlier, Japan had a long tradition of palm or hand healing during Usui's time; thus, Usui conceptualized his own healing system based on hand techniques.

Although the practice of Reiki healing is becoming popular these days, it was already used over a thousand years ago. According to history, the Tibetan Buddhist monks were the first to use the Reiki healing. However, in the late 1800's, Dr. Mikao Usui, a Japanese Buddhist rediscovered this holistic therapy and familiarized other people with its great benefits. He established the Usui system of Reiki, which is simple yet extremely efficient in healing the body, mind, and spirit. Usui's system has become the basis for today's practice of Reiki healing.

Reiki is an extraordinary method of channelling healing energy by an individual who have gone through the process of attunement. This process is similar to an initiation method in which an initiate is aligned with the life and healing energy of the Reiki through sacred symbols discovered by Mikao Usui. As soon as the initiate becomes attuned with the Reiki life energy, he or she is already empowered of channelling such energy to heal for the rest of his life.

The Reiki life energy is a healing energy, which goes through the practitioner or healer and is channelled to the recipient by a spirit guide. Given that the Reiki life energy is guided spiritually, it only affects the area where it is needed the most. Thus, it is regarded as an intelligent energy, which is used only for one's greater good. Moreover, the Reiki life energy cannot be misused or abused as it is only directed to where it is needed.

In general, individuals who carry out healing before going through the Reiki process of attunement will experience a change in the energies. It is important for an individual who wants to become a Reiki practitioner to go through the attunement process. This is because he needs to develop the intent to heal as well as learn where he needs to place his hands during healing. It is in the process of attunement that a practitioner learns to use the Reiki energy naturally and allow it to flow to where it is most needed.

The Propagation of Reiki Healing

In 1935, Hawayo Takata, a Japanese-American who was born in Hawaii travelled to Japan to consult Dr. Chujiro Hayashi about her serious health conditions. Dr. Hayashi was a disciple of Mikao Usui, making him well-known to treat various medical conditions using the Reiki system of natural healing.

Takata's first option was to obtain Western medical treatments; however, she decided to try Reiki healing. Takata was doubtful that Reiki healing could provide her with the treatment she needed because she had grave medical conditions. On the other hand, as soon as her Reiki treatment was successful, all her doubts disappeared and replaced by belief in the Reiki system of healing. She then decided to learn more about the Reiki system.

In 1937, Takata worked and trained at the clinic of Dr. Hayashi for two years prior to returning to Hawaii. Dr. Hayashi, on the other hand, followed Takata to conduct a lecture on the Reiki system. In his tour, Dr. Hayashi inducted Takata to the final level of attunement, making the latter a practitioner of the Reiki system.

Dr. Hayashi committed ritual suicide when the World War II broke. Meanwhile, Takata lost contact with other Reiki practitioners in Japan and feared that the death of Dr. Hayashi would also mean the death of Reiki healing in Japan.

After the war, Takata introduced the Reiki system of healing in the United States, Europe, and Canada. Given that the war left awful memories, particularly in Pearl Harbor, Takata found it difficult to teach the Reiki system in the Western countries. The aftermath of war made it extremely hard to bring in something that is related to Japan to the Western population. In her desire to introduce the Reiki system in the United States, Takata decided to modify the healing system in order to become acceptable to the population.

With this intention, Takata was compelled to make up a different story about the history of Reiki healing, which she presented to the Western population. She came up with a fabricated story that Mikao Usui was a Christian doctor instead of a Tendai Buddhist. Takata claimed that Usui travelled the world to explain the miracles of Jesus Christ and discover a healing system. Consequently, Takata's version of the history of Reiki healing began to spread in the Western countries.

Before her death in 1980, Takata was able to initiate twenty-two Reiki Masters. Many people who belonged to the Western population believed that Takata's version of the Reiki system was the only one in existence. However, some of the Western Reiki masters decided to travel to Japan. There, they discovered other practitioners who were applying the original healing techniques founded by Mikao Usui. The Western Reiki masters stayed in a small community that was inhabited by traditional Reiki masters.

In 2000, 12 Shinpiden students of Usui were found out to be alive and still practiced the original version of the Reiki system of healing. These students of Usui told the Western Reiki masters about the original history and structure of the Reiki system. Thus, the Reiki system was rediscovered and currently being taught and practiced in many Western countries.

Difference Between Traditional and Western Reiki Systems

Both the Japanese and the Western Style Reiki provide powerful and significant effects on the lives of practitioners. Both practices necessitate a commitment on the part of the practitioners for Reiki to help them on what they need. On the other hand, there are a few differences in how these two systems are carried out.

Western Style Reiki

Nowadays, many versions of Reiki are being taught and practiced all over the world. Some of the most commonly used are Usui Tibetan Reiki and Usui Shiki Ryoho, both focusing on the hands-on healing of the Reiki system. These styles or versions of Reiki are usually used for self-healing or healing others through touch.

Western Style or Modern Reiki is probably the most common version of Reiki taught in the United Kingdom and the United States of America. Hawayo Takata was responsible for introducing modern Reiki to the West. Takata learned the Reiki system from a Japanese teacher, Dr. Chujiro Hayashi.

Western Style or Modern Reiki is primarily focused on hands-on healing, which makes it merely as an external practice. It is as simple as connecting with the Reiki energy and channeling it to oneself or the recipient. However, although this is exactly the concept of Reiki, it is not as simple as it may seem based on its original teachings.

Although the hand positions for self-healing and hands-on healing of others in a Western Style Reiki session, the emphasis on the daily practice of self-healing is only little or limited. In fact, due to the increase of Reiki Masters centering their teachings on healing others, the self-healing part of Western Style Reiki is almost nonexistent. In addition, most cultures are used to extend a helping hand to others before they help themselves.

Western Style or Modern Reiki is also known for its teachings of balancing or adjusting the chakras, which are energy centers. Furthermore, in the second and third degree of Western Reiki, symbols and mantras are taught and used to alter the energy externally. There are symbols used for distant healing in which treatments are conducted from a distance.

In general, a degree or level of Western Style Reiki takes one to two days to teach. Depending of the lineage and on the Reiki Master, there can be 3 or 4 degrees or levels. On the other hand, the mastery of the healing is often missed or given little emphasis in Western Style Reiki. While it is true that the fundamental teachings of Reiki can take just a couple of days to teach, mastering of the healing system can take a long period.

Most people who have learned and experience Modern Reiki can testify that the system did many amazing things in their lives. Some say that Reiki came at a time that they needed it most while others say it caused their lives to change for the better.

On the other hand, some people who have learned Modern Reiki feel that there is something missing; that they need to learn other forms or styles of energy healing in order to have a better understanding of energy. Such missing part and understanding of healing energy can only be found in the original Japanese Reiki, founded by Misao Usui.

Japanese or Traditional Reiki

It is quite regrettable that the Japanese or Traditional Reiki was altered with fabricated stories about its true origins. Fortunately, many Reiki practitioners nowadays are seeking a deeper understanding of the concept of energy in the healing system. These practitioners long to discover a practice, which can aid them in finding out their true selves and living up to their one true purpose in life. As such, most of them have travelled all over the world, ended up in Japan, and rediscovered the Japanese or Traditional Reiki.

In its original structure, the primary focus of Reiki is on "the self" with the belief that only by learning to heal yourself, then you will be able to heal others. On the other hand, Reiki is more than just healing oneself and others. It is a spiritual practice that leads you to a deeper understanding of the interconnection between all entities and that the spiritual energy exists within and all around an individual.

To better understand the essence of Reiki, one of Usui's students recorded a quote from him that says, *"The training according to the natural law of this world develops human spirituality: the Universe exists in me, and I, exist in the Universe."*

In a Japanese Reiki course, you will be able to learn the energetic system that is centered on the Hara, which is also known as Tanden and Danden. Hara, in Reiki, is considered as the central energy powerhouse of the body. The literal meaning of Hara in Japanese is stomach, belly, or abdomen. It is believed to be the part of the body where energy is stored and that such energy flows throughout the entire body.

During a Japanese Reiki course, you will also learn to feel energy from the earth and the heavens, which is the energy system of the Japanese. You can attain this by learning to meditate using Reiki energy. The meditations involve integrated breathing techniques to aid in enhancing the Hara. The meditations are also very traditional and aimed at building the foundations for a stronger connection to the Reiki energy.

Similar to the Western Style Reiki, the second and third degrees/levels in Japanese Reiki teach both symbols and mantras. Then again, in Japanese Reiki, the symbols and mantras are viewed as training wheels. For instance, the symbols are visualized while the mantras are chanted. These practices result in having the right internal and external environments, causing the practitioner to feel and be the vibration of energy.

In addition, the Japanese Reiki gives more emphasis on the principles and how they work, which provides practitioners a genuine understanding of their nature.

Just like in Western Style Reiki, hand positions for self-healing and healing of others are also taught in Japanese Reiki. However, the hand positions are considered a framework that practitioners should develop upon. The purpose of this is to teach practitioners to work on intuition rather than depending on the framework. As practitioners work intuitively, the energy will guide them to where it is most necessary.

Science and the Reiki Therapy

During the 1980's, an independent research on the practice of healing therapies including the Reiki was conducted by Dr. John Zimmerman and Dr. Robert Becker. They found out that apart from the synchronization of the brain wave patterns in the alpha state, both the practitioner and receiver pulse in concurrence with the Schuman Resonance, the magnetic field of the earth. As the synchronization and pulsation transpire, the biomagnetic field of the practitioner's hands is increased by at least a thousand times more than normal. Furthermore, this increase does not result due to the internal current of the body.

Based on this research, other scientists have suggested that as the energy fields between the earth and the practitioner pulsate, the latter is enabled to draw on the universal energy field or the infinite energy source through the Schuman Resonance.

In 1991, Dr. John Gribben and Prof. Paul Davies discussed in The Matter Myth a "living universe" founded on the quantum physics view. They said that a "living universe" consisted of a living web of interdependence. This means that everything in a "living universe" is connected, supporting the subjective experience of "expanded consciousness" and "oneness" as claimed by people who receive Reiki regularly or self-treat with it.

Further investigations were made on the pulsating biomagnetic field between 1990 to 1992 both in the United States of America and Japan. These investigations discovered that while practitioners work, their hands of energy emit large pulsating biomagnetic field. They also discovered that the brain waves sweep up and down in the same frequencies as the pulses from 0.3 to 30 Hz, alpha state. In another independent medical research, the healing in the body is stimulated by this range of frequencies. Moreover, the research found out that there are specific frequencies suited for various tissues. For instance, 15 Hz stimulates capillary formation; 7 Hz stimulates bone growth; and 2 Hz stimulates nerve regeneration.

According to Dr. Becker, brain waves are not restricted to the brain. They travel all over the body through the perineural system, which comprises the sheaths of connective tissue around the nerves. In a practitioner during treatment, these waves may seem to be weak pulses in the brain's thalamus. However, they gather strength once they flow to the body's peripheral nerves including the hands. A person receiving treatment would also have the same effect. In addition, Becker suggested that this system is the most effective in terms of regulating system balance and injury repair. Thus, this system sets off one of the special characteristics of Reiki that both the practitioner and the receiver of the treatment experience the benefits, making it tremendously effective.

Interestingly, Dr. Becker conducted his study across cultural subjects all over the world and regardless of the customs or belief systems of his subjects, all tested the same. The growing popularity of Reiki is partly due to its neutrality, which means that it does not require any set of beliefs. Thus, it can be used by anybody or any faith or background. In addition, its neutrality is one factor that makes it appropriate for use in medical and therapeutic settings.

Reiki as a Gentle Therapy and an Energetic Radiance

Reiki Healing – A Gentle Therapy

While Reiki is a powerful and profound method of healing, it is also considered as a gentle and noninvasive therapy, which can reduce or eliminate stress, enhance the body's self-healing properties, provide relaxation, support the immune system, and replenish vitality. Unlike other types of natural healing, Reiki healing can be incorporated into traditional and modern medical and healing practices.

Many practitioners of Reiki healing claim that it is a holistic therapy because it works primarily through encouraging a healing response on the physical, mental, emotional, and spiritual spectrum of an individual. While other healing therapies only work on a physical level, Reiki healing can affect even the emotional issues of an individual. It also nourishes an improved sense of wholeness and balance in one's life. Reiki healing can also treat various physical disorders as well as nervous conditions. Consequently, Reiki healing is a gentle, holistic therapy that does not have negative side effects.

Reiki Healing – An Energetic Radiance

When Dr. Mikao Usui established his Reiki system of natural healing, his original intention was to use it primarily as a therapeutic method and self-development system. This intention involved the energy radiance that is found at the center of the Reiki system of natural healing. As mentioned earlier, the term "Rei" means universal, which is translated as spiritual or sacred. It is also known as the "soul." On the other hand, the term "Ki" means the life force energy. It can also imply "spiritedness" or feelings.

Thus, based on Usui's original intention, the Reiki system of natural healing can be construed according to the perspective of an individual. It can be universal, a life force energy, a spiritually-influenced life force energy, or an energetic healing radiance.

Reiki Healing Principles and Concepts

Reiki healing is based on a set of five principles, which is centered in helping an individual to change his attitude towards life. These principles encourage balance in an individual's soul as well as instill compassion regardless of one's situation.

The principles of Reiki healing have different translations; however, they all begin with the phrase, "Just for today" and end with the phrase, "for the improvement of the body and the soul." The five principles include 1) Just for today, do not worry; 2) Just for today, do not rise to anger; 3) Just for today, honor your parents, elders, and teachers, and manifest respect to all beings; 4) Just for today, be honest and diligent; and 5) Just for today, show gratitude to everything.

More often than not, these principles are intended to encourage goodness, blessings, and spiritual medicine for healing. They are usually applied every day and night while seated in a prayer position. The words are repeated out loud, coming from the heart of the individual.

In simple terms, these principles can be explained as:

Just for today – this indicates the significance of the present state, the "now," or "today." It entails that how one lives his/her "today" discerns whether or not he/she will go through and finish the required learning. This principle of "today" is an aggregation of moments that teaches one to live fully every moment and the entire day.

Do not worry – In order to fully trust the universe, an individual should go through the Reiki Mastership. This principle entails that one should not bear any unnecessary fear and worries. An individual should do his/her best "today" or in the present state and allow the universe to take care of everything. The principle also entails that an individual should keep the peace in his/her mind. By not worrying, one is also being free from worry or fear to trust in the univers and be with it as well.

Do not rise to anger – this indicates recover the balance of mind and emotion with the Reiki energy. It entails living a peaceful and quiet life. Furthermore, it instills that anger only hurts yourself as well as others.

Show gratitude to everything – An individual becomes thankful in a natural way when he/she receives the benefits of the Reiki as well as when he/she becomes familiare with the Reiki everyday.

Be honest and diligent – This principle entails that a dishonest and lazy mind is bad for an individual. By being honest and diligent, one will be able to grow and learn through everyday living.

Honor your parents, elders, and teachers, and manifest respect to all beings – This principle entails that a sense of oneness with the universe can be achieved naturally through the practice of love, that is, Reiki healing. It indicates that through cooperation of a huge number of people, a healthy society can be sustained. In addition, it entails that distinction does not exists between one's self and others in the universal dimension. What exists is only the establishement of the same soul. By being respectful and kind to one's self, one can also do the same with others.

Becoming a Reiki Healing Practitioner

In order to become a Reiki healing practitioner, the first prerequisite is to undergo a training that is structured according to levels. As mentioned earlier, anybody who wants to practice Reiki healing should go through the process of attunement or initiation, which involves transferring or channeling the subtle energy from a Reiki master to his student.

The first level of the Reiki training involves the process of attunement wherein the student is introduced to the Reiki energy flow. Level 1 provides emphasis on the hands-on therapy intended for self-treatment and treating others on a physical level. Therefore, the emphasis of Level 1 is on the outer or physical aspect.

The first level of the Reiki training also involves learning to "step out of the way" to allow the passage of the Reiki phenomenon. Level 1 is developing the ability to prevail over the desire of the conscious mind, which might hinder the natural process of healing. Simply put, Level 1 is learning to detach one's self from feelings, things, and circumstances, which may impede in the Reiki flow. It is learning to let go while letting the Reiki life energy flow.

The second level of the Reiki training allows an individual to intensify his quality of awareness of the Reiki flow. Symbolic tools are presented to the individual that would allow him to establish intentions and extend the therapeutic healing scope. In Level 2, an individual is introduced to three sacred symbols and taught how to use them for treating one's self and others on a psycho-emotional level. Level 2 also teaches an individual to become efficient in physical treatment as well as practice remote healing.

Finally, the third level of the Reiki training is known as the "Master" level. This is where an individual can already manifest his ability to transfer the Reiki life energy to others. In Level 3, the student will now become a full-fledged Reiki practitioner. Furthermore, in this level, the practitioner acquires a deeper connection with the Reiki energy flow. It is also where a fourth sacred symbol is introduced to the practitioner. This symbol is known as the Master symbol.

Distance Attunements

Just like Distance Healing, Reiki Masters also provide attunements distantly. Many Reiki Masters find this method extremely efficient especially for individuals who want to receive and be part of the Reiki system, but are not physically present to do so.

Prior to carrying out a distance attunement, Reiki Masters make sure to prepare the room to the allocated time with incense, music, and candles among others. Once it is time for the distance attunement, Reiki Masters state the following outloud or silently: "I now wish to give attunement to (name of individual) and (location) to Reiki Level (1, 2, or 3) or Master Level." Reiki Masters then pictures the student sitting in a chair inside the room and performs the attunement like the student is physically present in the room.

Regardless if Reiki Masters know or do not know how the individual looks like. The important thing is they are able to state their intent and the individual's name. More often than not, Reiki Masters conduct distance attunements during the day, specifically for Level 1, which has four attunements. Each attunement for Level 1 is carried out at different times of the day one after the other. Although it may take longer, it can save the student from going through the process four times.

After a Reiki Attunement

Once an individual goes through the process of a Reiki attunement and completes it, he/she: will be able to channel the Reiki energy through his/her hands to others and to one's self through connecting to the Reiki source; opens his/her chakras and is now connected to the unlimited source of the Reiki; becomes extremely aware of what he/she needs to do with respect to his/her healing; becomes more pyschic and intuitive; and experience more changes that are necessary and distinctive to him/her.

After the Level 2 attunement of the Reiki training, an individual will be able to manifest what he/she needs at a faster rate; his/her healing energy will be able to flow at a higher and stronger vibration; his/her awareness of the Reiki will expand continuously with his/her progress and experience; he/she will be able to use the three Reiki symbols, which include the *Cho Ku Rei, Sei He Ki,* and *Hon Sha Ze Sho Nen;* he/she will be able to know whent o use the Reiki symbols; he/she will be able to send the Reiki not only to the present state but also to the past; he/she will become more aware of the power of the Reiki as well as its intensity flow; and further changes will manifest, which is unique to the individual.

What to Expect in Reiki Classes

Individuals who are interested in joining Reiki classes can expect a number of teachings from Reiki Masters/Teachers, specifically those who are confident enough to pass attunements.

Some of the common teachings that students learn from the Reiki Masters include the story of the Reiki system of natural healing and what it is; the process of Reiki attunement; the process of cleansing after a Reiki attunement; the Reiki principles; how to carry out a Reiki treatment; the Reiki hand positions for treating one's self and others; the importance of energy exchange for services; and preparing for a Reiki attunement. More often than not, Reiki Masters provide their students with a list of Reiki books as well as manuals and handouts.

During the second level of the Reiki training, Reiki Masters/Teachers teach their students the nature and purpose of the Reiki symbols; how to use and practice the Reiki symbols; and the distance healing.

During the last level of the Reiki training, students are taught about the Reiki Master symbol as well as how to use it; the process of passing or giving attunements; what and how to teach classes in the different levels of Reiki training; the importance of an energy exchange for classes, attunements, and treatments. Students are also provided with handouts or manuals for the different levels of Reiki training.

CHAPTER 2

The Reiki Symbols

More often than not, traditional Reiki Masters avoid showing the Reiki Symbols to people who are not yet attuned, specifically to the second level of the Reiki training. It is believed that the symbols where made public in a book that was published in Australia. Still, it is up to the Reiki Master whether or not he/she will reveal the symbols to his/her students.

The *Cho Ku Rei* is the first symbol. It is regarded as the symbol of "power." Literally, it means "place the power her." It is a declaration to be awaken or to remember through letting go of things that hinder one from realizing his/her true nature.

The *Sei He Ki* is the second symbol. It is regarded as the "mental and emotional" symbol. It is also considered as the symbol for "harmony." This symbol emphasizes that one's focus should be in the present state and that each individual is believed to be a new creation at the present moment. The *Sei He Ki* is said to heal the mind, body, and spirit. It cleans and heals through eliminating the attachments that an individual has, which result in his/her illness or suffering.

The *Hon Sha Ze Sho Nen* is the third symbol. It is regarded as the "distant" symbol as well as the "connection" symbol. It is believed to come from a Buddhist chant, which means "a righteous man may correct all thought" or "right consciousness is the root of everything." Being in the right consciousness means being fully in the present state or in the present moment. Instead of "reacting," this symbol empha-sizes on "acting." Reacting depends upon one's ego or conditioning. More often than not, an individual's conditioning is the cause of his/her illness or suffering. Thus, by eliminating one's conditioning, he/she will be free to be in the present state in order to heal and respond.

These symbols are viewed as tools or a road map and not a destination or journey. In general, these symbols are activated by drawing each of them with one's finger/hand or one's mind. The symbol's name is either spoken out loud or just in one's mind, then visualizing to tap it three times. The pattern of activating the symbols is draw-name-tap-tap-tap.

The Power Symbol – *Cho Ku Rei*

The *Cho Ku Rei*, pronounced as sho-koo-ray is referred to as the power symbol or sometimes, the "light switch." This is because this symbol connects an individual to the energy similar to a switch when being turned on. The power symbol is said to make the energy come to surface while opening an individual to the Reiki energy channels.

The power symbol can aid in starting the flow of the Reiki. More often than not, practitioners use this symbol to begin their sessions by drawing it on their palms and hovering their hands to the air. Doing so is said to defeat negative patterns of resistance. Using this symbol on a particular area can lessen pain and clear spaces. The power symbol is also used for cleansing objects in an environment so that they can function for one's highest good. This symbol is drawn in an object to empower it with the Reiki energy.

Uses of the Power Symbol

The *Cho Ku Rei* is used for a number of purposes. Apart from starting a session to feel the connection between the Reiki source and energy, it is also used to center the power at each hand position as well as problem areas, if any. This symbol is also used by drawing it over an individual by the end of a session so that the healing energies would be sealed in.

Another use of the power symbol is to clear an area that is full of negative energies. For instance, the symbol is drawn to all the corners of a room, which is intended to be clear or filled with light.

The power symbol is also used for protection. This is done by drawing it on a paper and placing it under or on the things that are intended to be filled with the Reiki energy.

This symbol is also used during meditation by drawing it over on one's self. For instance, one can draw the *Cho Ku Rei* on a shower head before taking a bath. This allows the water to be filled with the Reiki energy while cleansing the individual.

Other Uses of the Power Symbol

Cho Ku Rei is also used to alter or enhance the taste and nutrients of food and drinks. This is done by putting the food or drink on top of the symbol for 10 minutes. Many can attest that there is a discernible difference in the taste of food or drink, which was placed above the power symbol. For instance, a cheap bottle of wine can taste better when it is placed on top of the power symbol prior to consumption.

Another use of the *Cho Ku Rei* is enhancing the function of objects. For example, when a battery runs low, drawing the symbol over it can increase its charge level.   Some people do this on their cell phone batteries. They draw the power symbol over their phones or their hands and the batteries increase their charge levels.

Cho Ku Rei is also used to make cut flowers last longer than simply putting in a vase with water. This is done by placing cut flowers in a vase. The individual should then hold the vase around its base in order to channel the Reiki energy. Drawing the power symbol on a paper and placing the vase on top can also make the cut flowers last longer.

The Mental and Emotional Symbol – *Sei He Ki*

The *Sei He Ki*, pronounced as say-hay-key is referred to as the mental and emotional symbol. It is also regarded as the symbol for harmony. This symbol is used for healing mental and emotional customs and habits than are no longer working for an individual. It is also used for fighting off mental and emotional distress.

Sei He Ki is also used for acknowledging emotional issues and healing them as well. It also promotes positive behavioral changes. In addition, this symbols helps in releasing negative conditioning brought by past experiences through responding instead of reacting. According to Buddhists, ego is caused by conditioning. Consequently, eliminating the conditioning of life results in the freedom of an individual from suffering. *Sei He Ki* heals and releases the desires and conditioning to obtain oneness and harmony.

Using the *Sei He Ki* for healing is quite simple. One can simply use it while healing with the basic hand positions. It is also used during emotional meditation for releasing and heal patterns and forms of conditioning, which cause problems and sufferings.

Reiki Treatments and the Sei He Ki

The energy frequency that *Sei He Ki* produces is higher than *Cho Ku Rei*. The *Sei He Ki* is used for generating balance between the emotional and mental planes. According to the surviving students of Usui, this energy of *Cho Ku Rei* creates a link with the spiritual which is why it is regarded as a celestial energy. Consequently, the energies from the mental and emotional planes are drawn together into harmony by the energy of the *Sei He Ki*.

When the *Sei He Ki* is drawn over one's body, there will be two effects. First, it enhances the energy flow through one's hands; and second, it directs the energy towards balancing the mental plane and releasing the emotional plane. Given that the *Sei He Ki* generates a high frequency, its effects are less discernible to the hands. In addition, although its energy is strong, it is finer and more delicate as compared to the energy of *Cho Ku Rei*.

The effects that *Sei He Ki* generates are diversified as the symbol is able to address tension, sleeplessness, traumas, stress, anxiety, and restlessness. It is also helpful in resolving emotional problems including anger and sorrow. This symbol is also efficient in releasing emotional blocks, which may be caused by unresolved issues that were not dealt with properly. Furthermore, this symbol is also used for improving or altering personality traits and undesirable traits.

The *Sei He Ki* is usually applied in areas such as the heart, head, and solar plexus, which are considered the primary mental and emotional centers. According to the traditional Chinese medicine, there are different emotions held in various organs of the body. For instance, fear is often held in one's kidneys; joy is held in one's heart; anger is held in one's liver; grief is held in one's lungs; and sympathy is held in one's spleen. As such, the energy of the *Sei He Ki* could be used specifically in those areas to address their imbalances and unwanted emotions. In Reiki, on the other hand, practitioners usually use their intuition to guide them to the areas that need healing.

Sei He Ki and Positive Affirmations

As one draws the *Sei He Ki* over the head, positive affirmations could also be used to help the subconscious mind accept one's intentions. Some of the most common affirmations include "you feel safe;" "you are loved;" and "you are calm, serene, and content" among others. There are a number of positive affirmations, which one could use as he/she works with the *Sei He Ki* on a specific area.

When using *Sei He Ki* with positive affirmations, practitioners start by sliding their hands underneath the head at the back of the client. The energy used comes from *Sei He Ki* through drawing it from above or visualizing the symbol over the client's head. Practitioners focus on the client's third eye as they pass along the positive affirmation or new thought pattern to the client. Others place one of their hands to the client's skull along the base while the other hand rests on the client's forehead.

Other Uses of the Mental and Emotional Symbol

Some other uses of the *Sei He Ki* include the following: 1) relationships – using the symbol as two related individuals lay in bed; 2) memory – using the symbol to remember such as when studying or preparing for a meeting; 3) goals – using the symbol to achieve one's plans, affirmations, ideas, and goals by writing them along with the symbol on a piece of paper; and 4) spirits – using the symbol to help lost souls or spirits travel "into the light."

The Distance Healing Symbol – *Hon Sha Ze Sho Nen*

Another aspect of the Reiki healing is the distance or absentee healing. Given that the Reiki system is a unique healing method, it is able to heal through the symbols, specifically the *Hon Sha Ze Sho Nen* even without the physical presence of the healer.

The distance healing symbol allows one to send his/her healing energies to other people at a distance. It is used specifically when applying the hand positions is inappropriate such as when the client is sexually abused or with a burn patient. In cases where hand positions are irrelevant, the Reiki energy is sent from across a room or at a distance. This is referred to as "beaming," which is used specifically in *Hon Sha Ze Sho Nen*. This symbol is also used for karmic release. It is able to send the Reiki energy outside of space and time.

The distance healing symbols is composed of five elements, which translate to "no past, present, or future." The only precept of *Hon Sha Ze Sho Nen* is "now" or the present state.

Hon Sha Ze Sho Nen, unlike *Cho Ku Rei* and *Sei He Ki*, does not generate energy at a specific frequently. It sends the Reiki energy in such a way that one does not have to worry about distance or time. The surviving students of Usui claim that the energy of the *Hon Sha Ze*

Sho Nen creates a state of mind that translates to "oneness;" that is, oneness with the universe, allowing a practitioner to transcend space and time.

The distance symbol is used to send the Reiki energy without putting one's hand to the client. It is able to send Reiki energy to someone in a different town, country, or continent.

Moreover, the surviving students of Usui claim that the distance symbol has various connotations. For instance, the associated kotodama is a "connection" kotodama, which allows one to send energy to another who seems to resist an emotional resist. For instance, one can visualize *Hon Sha Ze Sho Nen* over another's solar plexus to allow the emotions to connect and be released. In the event that the other person is need of improving how he/she expresses thoughts or emotions, a practitioner can visualize the distance symbol over the other's throat, heart, and solar plexus or throat to head in order to connect the emotional or mental areas with the center of communication. This may only take a few minutes given that the energy is not channeled as that with *Cho Ku Rei* and *Sei He Ki*. When starting a treatment using *Hon Sha Ze Sho Nen*, a practitioner rests his/her hands on another's shoulders. The practitioner also visualizes the *Hon Sha Ze Sho Nen* in his/her head while saying its name for three times. This way, the *Hon Sha Ze Sho Nen* connects with with the other person on a deep level or on all levels.

More often than not, using *Hon Sha Ze Sho Nen* for healing entails being guided by one's feelings instead of applying the symbol in an analytical or a calculated manner. It is important for the energy to flow and function when it deems appropriate.

Healing the Past

Just as the Reiki system of natural healing is efficient in healing the present state, it can also be sent to the past for dealing with difficult situations that left a mark. For instance, Reiki can heal a situation involving a regretful argument with a loved one that still has an effect in the present state. An individual would be able to deal with such situation that transpired in the past and heal its effect simply by imagining the situation and sending the Reiki through distant healing. Sending the Reiki to heal the past does not mean that one sends the Reiki "back in time." It means that one is healing the effect that the bad or difficult situation caused as well as how the individual interpreted the situation.

Sending the Reiki to the Future

One can send the Reiki to the future. For instance, if one would be having a job interview, he/she can send the Reiki to the place of interview ahead of the schedule. This way, the individual would be filled with the Reiki once he/she is already in the interview proper.

Drawing the Reiki Symbols

The following steps can help in drawing the Reiki symbols:

First, draw the symbol in different ways. Simultaneously, one should imagine that the symbol is being drawn in the color, violet, which is the most associated color with the Reiki. In the event that it is difficult for an individual to visualize colors, he/she can simply intend the symbol to be violet.

Second, the name of the symbol should be spoken to one's self three times. This should serve as a mantra.

Third, the drawn symbol should be tapped using one hand or finger while saying its name. There should be a total of three taps. This way, the symbol is activated and generates its appropriate effect.

The symbols are usually drawn in various ways. One, an individual can draw the symbol with the palm of his/her hand, where the energy comes out. This is applicable when drawing the symbol over a room's wall.

Second, an individual can draw the symbol over the body, making sure that all fingers and thumb form a cone. The symbol should be drawn over the hand or a part of the body. It is important to take note that the Reiki energy can also come out of one's fingers.

In the event that both hands are occupied, specifically when treating another person, a practitioner can trace the symbol, visualizing a Pinocchio-like nose. While imagining that the symbol is drawn through the "extremely long nose," the head movements used should be small.

Third, the symbol can be drawn using eye movements. A practitioner can trace the symbol over his/her hands or over a body part of a client or recipient.

When tapping the symbol, a practitioner can use his/her eyes or nose.

More often than not, an individual who mastered drawing the symbols is able to generate the desired effect simply through visualizing the symbols as a whole. Once the symbols become second nature to an individual, the latter can do away with drawing out the symbols.

CHAPTER 3

Uncommon Uses of the Reiki Symbols

There is no specific rule as to where one should use the Reiki symbols. As long as one feels that the symbols are of use to a particular circumstance or his/her intuition guides him/her to use the symbols, he/she may do so.

There are several uncommon ways that one can use the Reiki symbols.

The Power Symbol as a Filter

One can make use of the power symbol or the *Cho Ku Rei* as a filter for a number of things. These may include filtering negative thoughts, cleansing the organs, or keeping unwanted people out of one's mind among others. This technique starts by drawing the *Cho Ku Rei*, watching it hang or suspend in the air. The practitioner then asks his/her intuition the number of power symbols needed to deal with the specific issue. He/she also visualizes the number of power symbols that are suspended in the air.

The symbols are guided by the practitioner into his head to intending to clear and release negative thoughts. Practitioners also use the same steps when keeping people out of one's mind.

When the power symbol is used to filter one's body organs, the first thing to do is to draw the *Cho Ku Rei* and determine the number of power symbols required to cleanse one's organ. The practitioner visualizes the symbols being guided into the location of the organs while intending them to be cleansed.

More often than not, practitioners experiment on which method to use for a specific circumstance.

Reiki Symbols as Support for Interviews or Meetings

The mental and emotional symbol as well as the distance healing symbol may be used to help one deal with interviews or meetings. This method begins by drawing the *Sei He Ki* mentally between the practitioner and the recipient. The practitioner then intends that everything goes well with the interview or meeting and that the recipient performs his/her best during the said engagement.

In the same way, the recipient may receive the Reiki energy in advance through the distance symbol. The practitioner simply intends to fill the recipient with the Reiki energy once the latter is already in the interview or meeting.

Symbols as Tools for Cleansing a Room

The Reiki energy may also be used to cleanse a room that has negative energy. Prior to conducting a Reiki session with a client or recipient, it is important to clear and cleanse the room.

The method begins by activating all of the Reiki symbols in every corner of the room. This should be done three times while intending that the room be cleansed of all the negative energy it has. The practitioner may also intend to retain only the positive energy present in the room. In general, this method ends by activating all the Reiki symbols at the center of the room for three times with a similar intention.

Symbols as Self-confidence Boosters

This technique is specifically useful for people who feel that their self-confidence is low or diminishing. The practitioner asks the recipient to draw the power symbol in front of him/her. Then, the practitioner guides the recipient to step into the symbol and ask to boost his/her self-confidence as well as deal with the events of the day.

The Reiki symbols may be used in any possible way that one can imagine and for whatever purpose. For instance, one can use the *Cho Ku Rei* to clear the road ahead or clear traffic jams as he/she drives in a particular area. Some use the power symbol to ensure they have a parking space when they get to their destination. Others use the *Cho Ku Rei* to ensure that all drivers in front and behind them drives safely.

CHAPTER 4

The Reiki Master Level and the Master Symbol (Dai Ko Myo)

In this section, the focus will be on the Master level of the Reiki system as well as the *Dai Ko Myo*, which is regarded as the Master symbol.

As a teacher of the Reiki system of natural healing, one should be responsible for his/her own decisions, actions, and methods. As a teacher, one is his/her own Master and not of anyone else. This means that no teacher is responsible for the actions of another teacher whom he/she has attuned. The only responsibility of a teacher is to maintain the integrity of Reiki, specifically if it is integrated with other healing systems.

The Master Attunement

As mentioned earlier, the last level of attunement is the Master Level. Reaching this level is not yet the end of a practitioner's journey, but just the beginning. In the Master level, a practitioner would be able to make decisions, which one can never deem possible.

In the process of the Master attunement, the power, mental and emotional, distance, and master symbols are placed into the practitioner's hands and palms while he/she is in prayer position. There is only a single attunement in the Master level. Once done, the practitioner will be able to activate the Master symbol.

In addition, once the practitioner receives the attunement, he/she will be able to provide the levels of Reiki to other practitioners.

After a Reiki Master Attunement:

the healing energy will become stronger and vibrate at a more intense way; the healing energy will also expand continuously at the Master's pace; the Master's spiritual and personal growth will likewise expand to a higher level; the Master will become more connected with himself/herself as well as the universe; the Master will have a symbol that will enhance the other Reiki symbols; the Master symbol and attunement will help the Master in his/her own life as needed; the Master will become more spontaneous or intuitive; the Master's awareness with regard to the Reiki power's intensity will expand; the Master will develop a greater feeling of fulfillment and wholeness; the Master will experience various changes that are unique to him/her; all the Reiki qualities become enhanced through using the Master symbol.

Characteristics of Reiki Masters and Practitioners

Professional Conduct

Reiki Masters and practitioners think and act in an ethical and a professional manner. They perform only the services in which they are qualified. Reiki Masters and practitioners represent their professional affiliations, certification, education, and other qualifications in all honesty. In addition, Reiki Masters and practitioners do not declare themselves as psychotherapists or medical experts unless they are declared as such by their country or province.

Professional Appearance

Reiki Masters and practitioners give value to their professional appearance and cleanliness of self including their clothing, linens, office environment, and equipment among others. They strive for a relaxing professional atmosphere that involve clarity with regard to fees and reasonable scheduling.

Professional Excellence

Reiki Masters and practitioners are inclined to hone their professional excellence by conducting regular assessment of their professional and personal strengths and weaknesses. They also continue to train and educate themselves.

Professional Integrity

Reiki Masters and practitioners present the Reiki system of healing in a compassionate and professional manner. As they present Reiki, they are represent themselves as well as their practice in an ethical and accurate way. Reiki Masters and practitioners are honest when they are conducting their business. This means they prohibit themselves from providing fraudulent information to their clients. Reiki Masters and practitioners also forbid themselves from indicating any misrepresentation of who they are to their clients and students. They also do not act in a derogatory way, which might affect the nature and intention of the Reiki.

Health History/Referrals

Reiki Masters and practitioners make it a point to secure accurate client information, which includes profiles of the mind, body, and overall health history. They are keen in discussing with their clients any problem areas in which the use of Reiki is unsuitable. Reiki Masters and practitioners refer their clients to psychological or medical experts as needed.

Intention and Reliance

Reiki Masters and practitioners are expected to present their intention in facilitating therapeutic change that is holistic in nature. They are also expected to develop their capability to focus on the mind, body, and self. Reiki Masters and practitioners are encouraged to ask their clients questions about their well-being, which could institute and maintain a strong client relationship. In addition, they are expected to establish an atmosphere of safety as well as clear boundaries.

Communication and Privacy

Reiki Masters and practitioners make it a point to keep honest and clear communications with their clients. All information provided to them by their clients regardless if it is personal or medical are considered strictly confidential. Reiki Masters and practitioners also assure their clients that the techniques used for the Reiki healing are appropriate for every problem area. In addition, they only do the Reiki according to the range of their professional practice.

Equality

Reiki Masters are treated as equals regardless of their membership/ lack of membership or any association or body or their initiating Master. This premise is also the same for Reiki practitioners who are of the same level. Practitioners are treated as equals regardless of their belief system or initiating master.

Awareness

Reik Masters and practitioners avoid the abuse of drugs and alcohol. In fact, such substances are not used at all when they are conducting their professional activities.

Student Rights

Reiki Masters and Teachers make it a point to respect the rights of their students in terms of choosing their healing paths as well as their initiating master.

Respect of Clients

Reiki Masters and practitioners are expected to respect the physical and emotional states of their clients. They forbid themselves from abusing their clients through words, silence, or actions. In addition, they do not abuse their therapeutic relationship with their clients. For instance, Reiki Masters and practitioners do not in any way engage in sexual activities with their clients. This is because they regard the comfort zone of their clients for degree of pressure as well as for touch; thus, they honor the requests of the clients within professional, ethical, and personal boundaries. Furthermore, they recognize the individuality and inherent worth of each person; as such, Reiki Masters and practitioners do not discriminate against their clients and even their colleagues.

The *Dai Ko Myo* (Reiki Master Symbol)

The Reiki Master symbol is the *Dai Ko Myo*, which is pronounced as dye-ko-meoh. *Dai* entails great; *Ko* entails bright; and *Myo* means light. Some of the common uses of the Master symbol include: self-empowerment, increasing creativity and intuition; meditation; spiritual connection; harmonizing genetic and cellular healing; and rebalances the superior chakras including the throat, third eye, and crown chakras.

There are other specific uses of the *Dai Ko Myo*, which involves integrating it with the other Reiki symbols. For instance, the Master symbol can energize crystals by holding a crystal in one hand while using the other hand to draw the symbols in the following sequence: *Dai Ko Myo – Cho Ko Rei – Sei He Ki – Hon Sha Ze Sho Nen*.

The Master symbol is also used for stimulating mental clarity and learning by drawing the following symbols above the recipient's head in this order: *Dai Ko Myo – Cho Ko Rei – Dai Ko Myo*.

Distant healing is also possible through the use of the Master symbol either exclusively or integrated with the other Reiki symbols. *Dai Ko Myo* is applied to the recipient, having its name spelled for three times. The recipient would receive the treatment while his/her location is recognized. The practitioner then allows the Reiki energy to flow as required.

Reiki Masters and practitioners also use other combinations for distant healing including the following: *Dai Ko Myo – Cho Ku Rei*; *Dai Ko Myo – Hon Sha Ze Sho Nen – Sei He Ki – Cho Ko Rei*; and *Dai Ko Myo – Cho Ko Rei – Sei He Ki – Hon Sha Ze Sho Nen – Dai Ko Myo*.

These sequences are done in the same way as distance healing using the *Dai Ko Myo* alone.

The Master symbol is also used for karmic treatment. The practitioner holds his/her hands in front like a cup while visualizing the *Dai Ko Myo* between them. The symbol's name is spelled for three times and the recipient receives the treatment a the practitioner mentions to work on the karma. Then, the practitioner allows the Reiki energy to flow as needed.

Reiki Attunement: Preparation

A Reiki attunement is an empowerment process that opens a practitioner crown, heart, and palm chakras. It is likewise a process that connects a practitioner to the Reiki energy's unlimited source. During the attunement, there will be changes made by the Reiki energy to open a practitioner's system in order to channel the Reiki. The changes happen in the physical body, aura, and chakras. An emotional and release of toxins can transpire as part of the healing. In order for the attunement energies to work as well as create greater benefits, a process of purification is usually recommended.

Prior to receiving a Reiki attunement, a practitioner should avoid consuming alcohol, specifically the night before the empowerment process. He/she should only eat a light meal and as much as possible, avoid consuming red meat. As the attunement approaches, a practitioner should try to drink still water for cleansing his/her system.

A Reiki attunement is regarded as an initiation to the metaphysical, sacred order that is said to be present on Earth for over a thousand years. Through a Reiki attunement, a practitioner will become a member of a group of people who are utilizing the Reiki system both for healing themselves and each other. This group of people works together in order to heal the Earth in general. A practitioner who becomes a part of this group will also receive help from the Reiki Masters/Teachers and other spiritual beings who are likewise working to achieve these goals.

The Reiki Master Attunement

There are several steps in which Reiki Masters conduct an attunement to their students. The process of giving an attunement to students involves three parts, which should be completed by the Reiki Masters.

Part 1

> With eyes closed, the Reiki Master places both of his/her hands on the top of the student's head. The Master meditates briefly in order to develop an energetic rapport with the student.

> The Reiki Master touches the left shoulder of the student, indicating the latter to evoke his/her prayer. The Master's hands are clasped to the top of the student's head.

> Next, the Reiki Master draws the *Dai Ko Myo* over the student's head, repeating the symbol's name to himself/herself three times in mantra. The Master visualizes the symbol and guides it to his/her right hand, moving it into the student's Crown Chakra through the head and securing it to the brain's base.

> The Reiki Master then draws the *Cho Ku Rei* in the air over his/her hands, visualizing it to move into the hands down into

the Crown Chakra through the student's head and once again securing it to the brain's base. The Master mentions the power symbol to himself/herself three times as he/she places the symbol into the student's brain and hands.

In the same manner, the Reiki Master draws the *Sei He Ki* or the mental and emotional symbol followed by the *Hon Sha Ze Sho Nen* or the distance symbol.

The Reiki Master then moves the hands of the students gently from the top of the head and putting them back in front of the student's heart.

After which, the Reiki Master moves in front of the student.

Part II

The Reiki Master opens the hands of the students, making sure they are flat. Then, the Master holds the student's hands in his/her left hand if he/she is right-handed or to the right hand if he/she is left-handed.

Then, the Reiki Master draws the *Dai Ko Myo* in front of the Third Eye Chakra of the student while chanting the symbol's name three times. Simultaneously, the Master pictures it moving into the student's head through the Third Eye Chakra.

The Reiki Master does the same procedure as he/she draws the *Cho Ku Rei* (power symbol) followed by the *Hon Sha Ze Sho Nen* (mental and emotional symbol), then, the *Sei He Ki* (distance symbol).

With the Reiki Master's right hand, he/she draws the *Dai ko Myo* in the air, visualizing it to move into the hands. The Master chants the symbol's name to himself/herself three times and slapping the hands three times as well.

The Reiki Master does the same procedure as he draws the the *Cho Ku Rei* (power symbol) followed by the *Hon Sha Ze Sho Nen* (mental and emotional symbol), then, the *Sei He Ki* (distance symbol).

After which, the Reiki Master brings the hands of the student together, moving them in front of the Heart Chakra. The Master blows over the student's hands, the Third Eye and Crown Chakras, and back over the hands to the student's Solar Plexus Chakra, and back again to the hands.

The Reiki Master, then returns to the back of his/her student.

Part III

The Reiki Master places his/her hands on the shoulders of the student, looking down through the student's Crown Chakra and visualizing that the Heart Chakra can be seen. The Master places a positive affirmation to the Heart Chakra of the student through repeating it to himself/herself three times. Simultaneously, the Master intends that the subconscious mind of the student accepts it.

Then, the Reiki Master brings his/her hands together while placing his/her thumbs at the skull's base of the student. The Master repeats the following phrase as he visualizes a door with the *Cho Ku Rei* (power symbol) on it being closed and locked: "I am sealing this process with Divine Wisdom and Love." The Master intends and feels that the process is now sealed and complete. Consequently, the student connects directly to the Reiki source.

After which, the Reiki Master places his/her palms on the shoulders of the student, repeating the following affirmation: "Both of us are blessed by this attunement."

Then, the Reiki Master moves in front of the student, asking the latter to place his/her hands, palms down on his/her thighs. The Reiki Master instructs the student to breathe slowly and deeply as he/she opens his/her eyes.

The Reiki Master may add his/her own final blessing.

Although Reiki Masters differ in conducting the process of attunement to their students, the process discussed above is one of the most common ways of providing students with the empowerment process. There are various versions of the Reiki attunement process; however, they only have one purposes, that is, to empower students in the Reiki system.

CHAPTER 5

Benefits of Reiki Healing

Reiki healing is one of the most efficient and flexible healing systems because it can be incorporated with traditional and modern medical treatments. It is able to heal not only on a physical level, but also on the mental, emotional, and spiritual levels. This is because Reiki healing works through the transfer of the subtle energy, which provides balance in the body, mind, and spirit.

There are a number of holistic therapies today; however, the Reiki system of healing remains to be the most efficient given that it focuses solely on the energy of the body. It makes use of the universal life force that flows freely and abundantly, which provides the body, mind, emotion, and spirit the needed balance.

Primary Benefits of Reiki Healing

There are five primary benefits that Reiki healing can provide an individual. These include 1) offering cure or relief for various physical ailments; 2) preventing future illnesses or ailments; 3) providing balance and tranquility in the body, mind, spirit, and emotions; 4) aligning the chakras; and 5) being relevant to individuals of all ages.

Offering Cure or Relief to Various Physical Ailments

The Reiki system of natural healing can provide a cure or relief to different types of physical illnesses, complaints, or ailments. It increases the life force energy of an individual that flows freely throughout the body. The life force energy provides balance to an individual's organ system and improves the immune system to promote healing rather than merely addressing the symptoms.

Some of the physical health conditions that can be healed through a typical Reiki healing session include asthma, insomnia, migraine, arthritis, sciatica, chronic fatigue, and even menopausal symptoms. Furthermore, Reiki healing can help in promoting faster recovery, specifically for an individual who have gone through a surgery. When it comes to physical ailments, the Reiki system of healing can be incorporated with other medical practices without causing adverse effects on an individual.

Preventing Future Illnesses or Ailments

One of the best things about Reiki healing is that it not only cures or treats current and past ailments; but it can also prevent future ailments from occurring. Regardless if the ailment is physical, emotional, mental, or spiritual, Reiki healing does its job of curing an individual. On the other hand, Reiki healing cannot provide immortality to an individual. It only prevents potential ailments in various states.

Providing Balance And Tranquility In The Body, Mind, Spirit, And Emotions

Nowadays, most people face different responsibilities that are often burdensome. As such, people become stressed, causing their life force energy to get drained. While the body is tired and the mind is confused and unfocused due to different taxing circumstances, the tendency of an individual is to dwell on negative thoughts and feelings, which often result in mood swings. Consequently, an individual also finds it difficult to interact appropriately with other people. Reiki healing can bring back the body, mind, and emotions into a state of balance.

When an individual goes through regular Reiki healing sessions, his life force energy can be revitalized and the dispelled energies are likewise unified. Reiki healing provides an individual the opportunity to improve memory, obtain clarity of mind, and release negative emotions. These can result in stress and fatigue reduction, which in turn, provide an individual clarity of mind and allows him to make better decisions in terms of goal fulfillment. Through regular Reiki healing sessions, an individual can obtain happiness and inner peace. In addition, the immune system can also be improved given that stress is reduced or eliminated.

Aligning the Chakras

Chakras are energy centers, which are found within and all around entities. Although they could not be viewed physically, chakras are said to have tremendous effect on the body's system. For instance, if a chakra is blocked, the energy flow in an individual is obstructed. Accordingly, this may also result in physical, emotional, and mental disturbance. On the other hand, Reiki healing can open up chakras, tear down the blockages, and restore the chakras into a state of balance.

Being Relevant to Individuals of All Ages

Reiki healing is applicable to individuals of any age with physical, mental, emotional, or even spiritual problems. Even babies, toddlers, and the elderly can be treated using Reiki healing without the risk of complications or side effects. Young children, teenagers and adults are likewise entitled to the benefits of Reiki healing.

Secondary Benefits of Reiki Healing

There are benefits that Reiki healing can provide an individual. They may be secondary yet they are still significant in one's well-being through providing extraordinary outcomes. These benefits that help in healing any physical, mental, emotional, and spiritual problems include the following:

Physical/Mental

Reiki healing improves the body's natural healing abilities; reduces stress and encourages relaxation; ameliorates overall health; aids in having better sleep and rest; reduces levels of blood pressure; helps with chronic and acute problems such as asthma, injuries, eczema, and headaches among others; aids in cleaning the body from toxins; relieves symptoms and physical pain due to arthritis, migraine, and sciatica among others; removes blockages in the endocrine system; reduces side effects of medical procedures and medication; provides mental balance for memory, learning, and mental clarity; speeds up the process of recovery from surgery or long-term illness; brings balance and harmony among parts of the body; slows down the process of aging; increases vitality; increases the vibrational frequency of the body; and supports the immune system.

Emotional/Spiritual

Reiki healing provides balance in the mind and emotions; encourages harmony, peace, and spiritual growth; heals and strengthens personal relationships; provides relief for emotional distress/sorrow; provides a more peaceful state of being; improves capacity for empathy; and enhances one's ability to love.

Once Reiki healing takes effect, an individual is able to restore his natural healing ability. This is because Reiki healing provides the feeling of relaxation and frees an individual from stress and tension. Furthermore, participating in a whole-body Reiki healing session allows an individual to restore the general condition of his body. Reiki healing allows the body to deal and cope with anxiety, stress, and depression through opening the channels of energy. In addition, Reiki healing aids the body in addressing toxin buildup.

Individuals who are in good health can take advantage of Reiki healing as it can increase the innate defenses of the body. Consequently, an individual is able to demonstrate confidence and outward harmony in the daily circumstances in life. As such, an individual will have a better outlook in life. Reiki healing also provides additional energy that is needed if an individual is recovering from a surgery or certain illness.

A typical Reiki healing session can provide an individual with an extremely comfortable state of being that can manifest positive changes. The effects or benefits of Reiki healing can be reinforced by using it with other natural healing methods or therapies including meditation, aromatherapy, homeopathy, crystals, and Bach Flower remedies among others. Reiki healing can also be used as a complementary treatment with most medical procedures and practices.

For women, Reiki healing can be used even if they are pregnant as it can reduce pregnancy symptoms, which are often irritating and uncomfortable. On the other hand, men, children, and even plants and animals can take advantage of the benefits of Reiki healing for the improvement of their state of being.

The healing energy of Reiki can be used for discerning pain relief and releasing stress. It can also provide quick energy regardless of time and place.

Other Benefits of Reiki Healing

Apart from healing human beings, Reiki can also be used for treating animals. A number of Reiki practitioners have asserted that animals are able to respond well to Reiki. One reason for this is that animals do not have a pre-conceived ideas of the Reiki energy. In addition, treating animals can provide a boost to a Reiki practitioner.

More often than not, animals require lesser time for Reiki treatment as compared to people. A reiki practitioner may experience that after several minutes, animals may walk away naturally as they have already received the sufficient Reiki energy they need.

When treating animals, a Reiki practitioner places one of his/her hands on the head of the animal while the other hand on the chest area. This allows the animal to settle or become steady. Then, the Reiki practitioner allows the Reiki to flow while maintaining the same position. The energy will surely find its way to the area where it is most needed. Some animals may manifest happiness as they receive Reiki for long periods. Most, on the other hand, will be happy even with just a 5-minute Reiki treatment.

A Reiki practitioner who intends to treat an animal that is not tame sits near it while holding out his/her hands. The practitioner intends for the Reiki to flow from his/her hands to the animal. The same procedure is done for a bird that is not tame. The practitioner simply sits as close as possible to the animal while holding out his/her hands and with the intention that the animal receives the Reiki energy.

Reiki healing can also be used for grounding. Once an individual completes his/her healing, he/she should be able to ground himself/ herself. This is done by clasping one's hands together and saying, "I am grounded."

There is also another technique, which can be used for grounding one's self. It is recommended that the technique be practiced each day on one's self. To begin, one should sit in a chair with his/her feet laid firmly on the floor. With eyes closed, the individual should be able to picture tree roots coming out of his/her feet's soles and going down in the earth's center. The individual should also be able to picture a white light that comes in through the top of his/her head, going down through each chakra, and coming out through the roots into the earth. This cycle should transpire for as long as the individual feels necessary. After which, the individual can already open his/her eyes.

CHAPTER 6

How Reiki Healing Works

In general, the concept of the Reiki system of natural healing is transferring the life force energy from a Reiki master or practitioner to another person. The hands of the Reiki master or practitioner become the passage of the life force energy to be directed to specific points of an individual to facilitate healing or recovery.

There are some instances when Reiki healing is practiced or applied at a distance. This means that the recipient of the healing is not physically present with the Reiki master or practitioner.

On the other hand, people who are interested in the Reiki system of natural healing should keep in mind that it is not a psychic surgery, religious cult, medical technique, form of mind control, Shamanism, imagination, diagnosis method, massage technique, or psychotherapy.

Given that the Reiki may be difficult to understand in terms of how it truly works, an individual should not force himself/herself. In reality, nobody veritably knows who the Reiki system works; however, it would still work whether or not an individual understands it. The important thing is that the individual's life will be changed in the most positive way.

In addition, it would greatly help to understand how the Reiki works if he/she continuously practices it.

How Reiki Healing Works: The Theory

As mentioned in the previous chapters of this book, Reiki healing works through transferring the subtle energy or the life force energy that is infinite and present within and all around entities. The subtle energy is formed into energy systems and fields within individuals and between the environment and entities. The energy systems allow the subtle energy to be transferred or channeled from one individual to another.

The subtle energy is transferred or channeled from a Reiki master or practitioner to another individual in order to activate and ameliorate natural healing abilities. The subtle energy can also be transferred or channeled to other entities aside from human beings. Even plants and animals can receive the subtle energy in Reiki healing.

The subtle energy or the life force energy that Reiki healing provides an individual can offer a balance between the body and the mind. This is what makes Reiki healing a holistic healing method. However, some researchers who have studied the concept of the Reiki healing claim that the subtle energy does not exist and that Reiki healing only emphasizes on the effects of the subtle energy instead of its existence.

When it comes to the Reiki system of healing, the term "illness" does not necessarily mean a health disorder or issue. Illness in the Reiki system is a blockage in an individual's energy field. Reiki healing brings balance back, which results in health improvement in a physical level. Reiki masters or practitioners undergo an extensive training in order to learn how to open and determine the availability of the subtle energy.

Reiki masters or practitioners do not need a conscious effort in order to activate the healing effects of the Reiki system. As such, it becomes a fact that Reiki healing does not come from the Reiki master or practitioner as the system itself facilitates the process of opening the self-healing abilities of an individual.

In addition, Reiki healing does not necessitate any anatomical or physiological background on the part of a Reiki master or practitioner. It does not call for a previous knowledge in manipulation or massage techniques. The only requirement when practicing Reiki healing is the intention to heal.

How Reiki Healing is Done: The Healing Session

Based on Usui's original Reiki system of natural healing, the practice involves 12 hand positions, which address the main chakras of the head and trunk. Reiki healing also involves the use of an approach that addresses an individual from head to toe. Accordingly, Reiki healing makes use of a designated set of hand positions, which covers different parts of the body while the recipient is lying down, standing, or sitting and fully clothed. As mentioned earlier, Reiki healing can also be practiced even if the recipient is not physically present with the Reiki master or practitioner during a session.

At the beginning of the Reiki healing session, the hands of the Reiki master remain in each appointed position for at least five minutes. In general, a Reiki master follows his intuition as to where his hands will be placed in order for the subtle energy to flow at a specific position. When treating others, a Reiki master positions himself/herself just above the head of a table or bed and begins the designated hand positions for the head. The Reiki master then moves his hands gently down the individual's body and returns to the affected area after some time.

For the entire duration of a Reiki healing session, a Reiki master may use ten to twenty hand positions depending on the needs of the recipient. Some advanced Reiki practitioners change the order of the hand positions to allow the spontaneity of the subtle energy flow in the individual's body. In general, a Reiki session lasts for one and a half to two hours.

As discussed in Chapter 1 of this book, in order to become a Reiki master or practitioner, one should first complete the three levels of attunement. During the training or attunement, the only requirement is the individual's desire to learn, heal, and offer commitment in using the Reiki system of healing according to its original form. Reiki can be learned, practiced, and access by everyone; however, an individual may be hindered from connecting with the subtle energy due to a history of physical, mental, or emotional distress. This is the reason why each level of the Reiki attunement involves a set of training methods for opening up blocked energy fields as well as enhancing the energy channels of an individual who wish to be a Reiki master or practitioner.

Originally, the Reiki system of natural healing was taught verbally, which means that it can be learned through an individual's intuition and guidance from a Reiki master. During Usui's time, there were no textbooks or any tangible material to guide those who want to learn the Reiki system. This is why the Reiki system had a number of versions through the years.

Today, there are several Reiki organizations that have established their own protocols for the three levels of attunement. The protocols are usually facilitated by a Reiki master who has reached and finished the attunement process.

How Reiki Healing Changes Lives: The Effect

Reiki healing is said to have the ability to change one's life in an intense way due to its overwhelming effects. These effects begin once an individual decides to learn as well as devote himself/herself to using the Reiki system.

The Reiki system of natural healing paves the way for new horizons to affect an individual's physical, emotional, mental, and spiritual levels. Reiki healing offers the ability to see people, things, and circumstances positively no matter what the situation is. For example, once an individual experiences the art of Reiki healing, he can perceive an insignificant grievance just the way it is rather than dwelling on it, affecting his emotions. Reiki healing can unblock and relieve the mind of an individual from tension and stress, allowing him to look at life's bigger picture. In other words, Reiki healing is able to change one's life simply by setting an individual free from negativity in physical, mental, emotional, and spiritual levels.

Reiki healing is said to be a powerful method that arouses the perspective of an individual in terms of his ultimate purpose in life. It allows an individual to have clear thoughts, actions, and emotions, affirming his natural ability to heal as well as be healed.

Reiki healing is also said to change one's life when he realizes his spiritual self. Reiki healing does this through the life force energy. In addition, Reiki healing allows an individual to be free from any inhibition. It also allows an individual to develop clarity in both the mind and emotions.

When an individual regularly practices or receives Reiki healing, he will experience significant changes in his life. At first, these changes may be irrelevant; however, they will eventually affect an individual's entire state of being positively in the long run.

More detailed information on how Reiki healing can change one's life will be discussed in Chapter 7 of this book.

The Significance of an Energy Exchange

Dr. Mikao Usui learned about the significance of an energy exchange after his experience in the Beggar's Quarters in Kyoto. When is was empowered to carry out miracle healings, which he sought for a long time, he thought to move to the Beggar's Quarters and be of service to the poor. Dr. Usui had the intention to help heal the poor in order for them to become responsible citizens. He also wanted to help the poor in enabling themselves to have a job for supporting themselves.

During his stay in the Beggar's Quarters, he discovered that many of the poor returned after experiencing the life outside. They decided that it was not for them to be responsible in caring for themselves. As such, Dr. Usui impressed the beggar pattern in most of the poor through providing healings.

Dr. Usui asserted that to fully appreciate what people are given, they need to give back whatever they receive. Consequently, he discovered two significant factors. One, an individual should initiate on receiving a healing. This translates that a healer does not have the job to try or help an individual who is not willing to receive healing. Two, Usui discovered that an energy exchange is necessary for the healer's time. This translates that it is not proper for a healer to make an individual feel indebted for the services given to him/her; as such, the receiver frees himself/herself of being obligated through sharing various forms of energy and has an investment in the outcome.

The energy exchange is not necessarily limited to being in the form of money. Usui prefers that an exchange of energy should be a trade. For instance, if an individual is a family member, an energy exchange transpires all the time; thus, there should not be a request for a certain compensation.

In Reiki classes, an exchange of energy should transpire. For instance, a Reiki Master should not waste energy and time sharing invaluable information or sharing information to those who are not prepared or interested to receive one.

The concept of tithing is another aspect of an energy exchange. Tithing refers to a sharing of what one has with others. It is sort of giving back and expressing gratitude to the Universe for what one has received. Tithing should be done with a deep sense of Love rather than out of obligation. When an individual does tithing because he/she is obligated, it would not have a profound effect.

CHAPTER 7

Reiki Healing and the Chakras

Chakras Explained

Chakras are known the entryway into one's aura. The term, "chakra" in Sanskrit translates to the act of "wheeling." In the Reiki system of natural healing, chakras are known as the energy centers, which receive, absorb, and channel the subtle energy or the life force energy. Chakras are responsible for the physical, mental, emotional, and spiritual aspects of an individual. Chakras are not only for human beings. They also receive, absorb, and channel energy to and from the universe, nature, celestial entities, and non-living things.

According to ancient writings and studies, the body of a human being comprises of 88,000 chakras that are all over the areas of the body. The majority of these chakras is insignificant; however, 40 chakras are said to have substantial functions, specifically those found in the hands, feet, shoulders, and fingertips. Consequently, seven out of the 40 chakras are said to be the most important ones. These are referred to as the Seven Major Chakras that are situated along the central line of the body; that is, from the base of the spine to the top of the head. These seven chakras are located in the supernal or ethereal body affirm the spiritual energy based on a physical level.

Meanwhile, the aura refers to the luminous body of energy, which enshrouds and goes through an individual. The aura encompasses at least seven layers, each dealing with various aspects of a person's state or being. The aura receives and emits energy through the chakras. The Seven Major Chakras stretches out like a cone from the core of the spine, penetrating all the layers of the aura.

Each of the Seven Major Chakras corresponds to the endocrine grandular system of an individual. This system is responsible for regulating the body's hormones. On the other hand, the hormones contribute to the general health and well-being of an individual. As a matter of fact, hormone regulation manipulates some of the most substantial processes in one's body, including growth, stress reactions, healing, aging, and reproductive systems. All these processes are associated with the secretion of hormones in the endocrine system.

Consequently, the role of the chakras is to align the seven major endocrine glands. Thus, during a Reiki healing session, the endocrine glands, which encompass the chakras are satiated with the subtle energy or the life force energy in order to obtain or bring back balance.

Chakras can affect the daily life of an individual. Similarly, a positive experience can bear on an individual's state of his chakras positively. On the other hand, a negative experience can disrupt the state of an individual's chakras and result in an imbalance. For example, when a person receives a hug from another person, it can affect his heart and sacral chakras positively. In turn, these chakras will obtain beneficial energy and diffuse it evenly. Consequently, the individual will become happy and feel loved.

In the same way, if a person experiences a negative event such as a death in his family, the chakras can be disrupted. Once the chakras are disrupted, the individual will feel unpleasant and uncomfortable.

It is important that the chakras are balanced. They should always move in a circular motion to bring about a feeling of wholeness as well as contentment. A chakra that functions well will result in better health and vitality. Meanwhile, a chakra that functions weakly and is imbalanced will result in depression, lack of energy, and restlessness.

The Seven Major Chakras

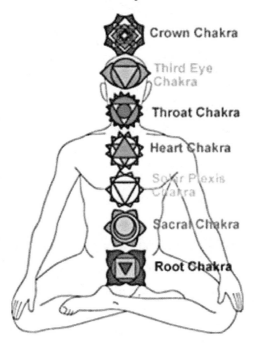

First Chakra – Root

In Sanskrit, the first chakra is known as the Muladhara. The root chakra is located between the pubic bone and the tailbone. It holds the basic needs for security, safety, and survival. The root chakra is responsible to where an individual comes from; that is, family relationships or tribal affiliations. It also regulates the physical identity, family/social honor, and instincts of an individual. When there is balance in the root chakra, it can offer a person with a sense of being grounded to the Earth. When there is imbalance, the root chakra can manifest fatigue, low energy, obesity, recklessness, and greed. The root chakra is associated with the earth element; the color red; and the sense of smell.

Second Chakra – Belly (Sacral)

In Sanskrit, it is known as the Svadisthana. The second/sacral chakra can be found below the navel (about 2 inches below); it is rooted into the spine. It regulates one's self-gratification, creativity, sexual energy, additions, movement, desires, and physical sensations. The sacral chakra is responsible with an individual's relationship with other people. It also keeps people connected through their emotions or feelings as it can provide the ability to offer and receive intimacy, sensuality, and creativity at different levels. When there is balance in the sacral chakra, it can ameliorate a person's relationship and connection with others. When there is imbalance, the sacral chakra can manifest promiscuity, frigidity, and impotence and impede creativity. The sacral chakra is associated with the water element; the color orange; the musical note of D; and the sense of taste.

Third Chakra – Solar Plexus

This is also known as the Solar Plexus Chakra. In Sanskrit, it is known as the Manipura. The solar plexus chakra is located between two inches below the breastbone or just above the navel. It is the center of an individual's relationship with himself/herself. The solar plexus chakra is responsible for an individual's personality, self-esteem, ego, and intuition. When there is balance in the solar plexus chakra, it allows an individual to achieve his goals easily and determine his will and personal desires. When there is imbalance, the solar plexus chakra can manifest high levels of stress, aggression, complacency, and control issues. It is also associated with an individual's self-honor, self-definition, opinion formation, introversion, personal power, fears, and anxiety. The solar plexus chakra is associated with the fire element; the color yellow; the musical note of E; and the sense of sight.

Fourth Chakra – Heart

In Sanskrit, the fourth chakra is known as the Anahata. The heart chakra can be found between the shoulder blades, along the spine in the back, behind the breast bone. It is at the center of the chest. It is the center of an individual's love, spirituality, and compassion. The heart chakra is responsible for the union of energies between a man and a woman. When there is balance in the heart chakra, it can offer a person with the feeling of peace. It can also nurture strengths, be in harmony with one's self and other people, and follow the impulse of the heart. When there is imbalance, the heart chakra can manifest distrust, smothering, emotional imbalance, and codependency. The heart chakra is associated with the air element; the color green; the musical note of F; and the sense of touch.

Fifth Chakra – Throat

In Sanskrit, the fifth chakra is known as the Vishudda. It can be found in the V-shaped area where the collarbones meet at the lower neck or in the body's mouth and neck areas. It is the center of an individual's growth and communication. The throat chakra is responsible for the ability of an individual to change, transform, and heal. It is also the center for sound vibration, fluent thoughts, independence, language, and self-expression. When there is balance in the throat chakra, it allows a person to organize and connect thoughts and emotions and prefer compassion over judgment either of self or others. When there is imbalance, the throat chakra can manifest the inability to listen and speak and make clear choices. It can also cause an individual to talk too much and become disputative. The throat chakra is associated with the ether element; the color blue; the musical note of G; and the senses of hearing and speaking.

Sixth Chakra – Brow/Third Eye

The sixth chakra is known as the Brow/Third Eye Chakra. In Sanskrit, it is known as the Anja. The brow/third eye chakra is located between the eyebrows or above the physical eyes on the forehead's center. It holds an individual's ability to trust his inner intuition or guidance. The brow/third eye chakra is responsible balancing the lower and higher self. When there is balance in the brow/third eye chakra, it can offer a person the sense of truth and self-reflection and seeing things in a bigger picture. When there is imbalance, the heart chakra can manifest forgetfulness, racing thoughts, inability to recall dreams, being illogical, and headaches or migraines. The brow/third eye chakra is associated with the air element; the color purple/indigo; the musical note of A; and the senses of sight and extra sensory perception (ESP).

Seventh Chakra – Crown

In Sanskrit, the seventh chakra is known as the Saharara. The crown chakra is located on the top of the head or behind the skull's top. It holds an individual's Divine self-knowledge, universal identity, pure consciousness, highest thought, and connection to the greater world beyond. It connects all other chakras through honoring a higher power. When there is balance in the crown chakra, it can offer a person the sense living in the present and seeking truth, wisdom, and clarity. When there is imbalance, the crown chakra can manifest lack of spiritual awareness, lack of higher purpose, and the feeling of disoriented. The crown chakra is associated with the light element; the colors violet and white; and the musical note of B.

CHAPTER 8

Reiki Healing Hand Positions for a Healthier and Better Life

A Reiki healing session involves a Reiki master or practitioner positioning his hands on the body of the recipient in order to channel the subtle energy or the life force energy. Although the healing session may be simple, its effects are very significant. During a Reiki healing session, there is an exchange of energy between the Reiki master and the recipient. The Reiki energy channeled from the Reiki master to the recipient knows what to do and where it is most needed.

In general, a typical Reiki healing session encompasses a designated set of hand positions that are well-spaced and placed along the body of the recipient. The hand positions guarantee the most favorable coverage to where the life force energy is most needed. In addition, traditional Reiki masters or practitioners only use their intuition to determine where their hands should be positioned for a particular ailment or issue when healing themselves or other individuals.

A Reiki healing session covers almost all body parts and the Seven Major Chakras. More often than not, Reiki masters or practitioners spend additional time on the parts of the body that draw out more energies. In addition, some Reiki masters or practitioners apply variations to the basic hand positions.

The next section is about the different hand positions for self-treatment and treating others in order to obtain a healthier and better life as well as relieving any form of illness, stress, and pain, regardless if it is on a physical, mental, emotional, or spiritual level. These hand positions are also designed to increase one's energy and have a sense of self-appreciation. In general, the hand positions used in Reiki healing are designed to heal or improve various body parts as well as other issues related to one's state of being.

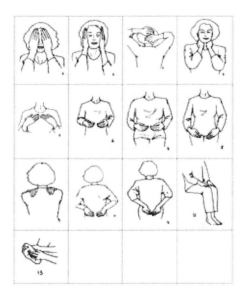

Reiki Healing Hand Positions for Self-Treatment

Head

The first position for self-treatment is covering your eyes using the palms of your hands. Make sure that you are able to touch your eyes as lightly and gently as possible. The second position is covering your ears using the palms of your hands. The third position is placing your hands on the back of your head, side by side or one hand on top of the other.

Front of the Body

The fourth position is putting your hands on both the sides of your neck. The fifth position is placing one of your hands on your chest just above the breasts. Then, place your other hand on top of your breasts towards your neck. The sixth position is putting your hands under your breasts directly towards the solar plexus. The seventh position is putting your hands on your abdomen, a few inches above your stomach. The eight position is forming a V-shape with your hands. Your fingers should be slightly touching each other. For men, the fingers should be below their waist while for women, the fingers should touch the area where their ovaries are.

Back of the Body

The ninth position is putting your hands on your shoulders with your fingers bent and pointing towards your shoulder blades. The tenth position is putting your hands on your back upon your waist. Your palms should be on both the sides of your spine. Make sure that you do this at a comfortable distance. The eleventh position is putting your hands on your back upon your hips.

Legs and Feet

The twelfth position is putting your hands upon your knees. Then, use your hands to cup your feet.

Reiki Healing Hand Positions for Treating Others

Face The first position is putting your hands over the face of the recipient, specifically on his forehead as lightly as possible. Your fingers should cup the eyes of the recipient. The recipient's airways of his nostrils should not be covered. Avoid constricting the breathing of the recipient.

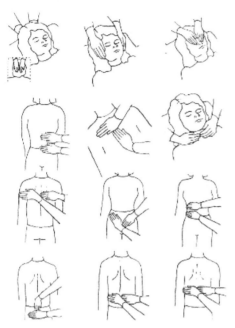

Crown and Top of the Head

The second position is wrapping your hands around the recipient's head. Your inner wrists should touch each other. Your fingertips should touch the ears of the recipient.

Back of the Head

The third position is tucking your hands under the recipient's head. Form your hands into a comfortable cradle as you take the head of the recipient. Your hands should be in a relaxed position. You can do this by resting them on a pillow or massage table.

Chin and Jaw Line

The fourth position is cupping your hands on the recipient's jaw line. Your fingers should touch each other under the recipient's chin. The heels of your hands should rest lightly over the ears of the recipient.

Heart and Neck Collarbone

The fifth position is wrapping your right hand on the recipient's neck as gently as possible. If the recipient becomes uncomfortable, hover your hand slightly above his neck. Place your left hand over the heart of the recipients. Make sure your left arm is stretched and your left hand is placed at the center of the recipient's heart.

Ribs and Rib Cage

The sixth position is putting your hands on the recipient of the upper rib cage right below the breasts of the recipient. Naturally, you should not touch any private area of the recipient.

Abdomen

The seventh position is putting your hands directly on the solar plexus of the recipient just above his navel.

Pelvic Bones

The eighth position is putting your hands over each side of the pelvic bone of the recipient. You can tell the recipient to change his position in a comfortable way. The initial position of the recipient should be lying on his back. Make sure to help him to switch to lying on his stomach.

Shoulder Blades

The ninth position is putting your hands on the shoulder blades of the recipient. The shoulder blades are where negative emotions are stored. Keep your palms on the recipient's shoulder blades for a longer time in order to aid the recipient in unblocking negative energies. This will eventually release his emotional burdens.

Mid Back

The tenth position is putting your hands in the middle back area of the recipient.

Lower Back

The eleventh position is putting your hands on the recipient's lower back, continuing to treat the back part of his body.

Sacrum

The twelfth position is using your hands to "comb" the recipient's aura. This eliminates any blockage or energy debris that was lifted from the physical body of the recipient during the healing session.

CHAPTER 9

Reiki Healing and the Process of Positive Changes

Reiki healing is essentially a system, which involves a positive change that transpires when an individual changes his beliefs, perceptions, and attitudes towards one's self, other people, the world, and the universe. It is a fact that most physical, mental, emotional, and even spiritual problems are outcomes of internal agitation, which result from an individual's inability to balance the various parts of his being as well as his past and present life. In addition, physical pains, illnesses, and diseases are indications that an individual is not in harmony with himself.

Accordingly, true self-healing demands of being committed to changing the way one thinks and feels. There are some attitudes that may be changed through learning as well as understanding a specific truth about one's self. On the other hand, there are attitudes that may be profoundly instilled in an individual.

A great deal of positive change may be acquired through Reiki healing coupled with meditation, reflection, prayer, and determination to think, act, and feel in a better way. A huge part of the Reiki system of natural healing is learning and understanding the truth about one's beliefs, perceptions, and attitudes and becoming prepared and willing to alter them.

One of the most significant benefits of Reiki healing is allowing an individual to guide his life in a manner that is most appropriate for him. Focusing Reiki healing on difficult circumstances in life allows an individual to be guided on what to do more easily. Once the life force energy is channeled to an individual, he may feel an improvement in his present state. This is similar to having a fresh perspective about life.

Most Reiki masters and practitioners attest that the flow of the Reiki healing energy has helped them in developing and strengthening their character. Thus, they are able to deal with difficult situations in a more positive and appropriate way. Apart from providing pertinent information, Reiki healing also provides the right kind of energy that an individual needs in order to change his perspective about life in a positive way.

Through using the power of Reiki healing, an individual will be able to deal with his actions more easily and become responsible for them. The healing energy of Reiki guides an individual to balance his personal energy in a way that is healthy not only for himself but for all entities around him.

CHAPTER 10

Emotional Healing Meditation using Reiki

More often than not, the mental and emotional symbol, *Sei He Ki* is used for emotional healing. In this meditation technique, however, all the Reiki symbols are used to experience an ultimate emotional healing.

To start the meditation, you may sit in a chair in which you are comfortable with, then relax. If you are uneasy, it is best to perform a systematic muscular relaxation method. One method you can use is allowing your feet to be the source of relaxation. Allow the sensation to move up to your legs, feeling your bones and muscles relax. The sensation you feel is the energy that moves up your legs and into your calves until it reaches your knees and thighs. Make sure your legs remain relaxed while allowing the energy to move up into your hips. By now, both your legs and thighs should be relaxed while letting the energy move up your spine. You should feel a warm sensation move up your spine, relaxing the muscles in your back. Then, allow the energy to move into your shoulders, down to your hands, and into your hands. Once all these body parts are relaxed, allow the energy to flow into your upper arms, forearms, and hands. The energy should then move up to your neck then up your head, and into your scalp. Allow the energy to move down over your forehead and into your jaw. Now, you should feel completely relaxed as you let the energy from your feet flow all throughout your body. You may now proceed with the emotional healing meditation.

In this meditation techniques, the symbols used are *Cho Ku Rei, Sei He Ki,* and *Hon Sha Ze Sho Nen.*

Since your entire body is already relaxed, take note of all your emotional issues and become aware of them. It is best to concentrate on how you feel regarding those issues.

Then, visualize the *Cho Ku Rei* symbol drawn in front of you, on your palms, and above your crown. Use a similar technique with the *Hon Sha Ze Sho Nen.* Then, draw the *Sei He Ki* in front of you, making sure that you are still aware of your emotional issues as well as the feelings you have for those issues.

Once you brought the issues into awareness, draw and visualize the *Sei He Ki* over the issues. You should be able to meditate on the mental and emotional symbol while feeling it heal you. At this point, the *Sei He Ki* is already functioning to heal your emotions for your highest good.

Next, draw the power symbol (*Cho Ku Rei*), the distant healing symbol (*Hon Sha Ze Sho Nen*), and the mental and emotional symbol (*Sei He Ki*) while connecting them to a particular emotional issue. Focus on healing yourself emotionally by taking note of when and how the issue transpired. Send healing within the past that continuously lingers and creates emotional burden. You can use an affirmation such as "I release this burden for my highest good" or "I am healed." you can also think of anything that would help during the process of healing. State the affirmation three times as you meditate on the universal love and harmony, which the *Sei He Ki* represents. Let the mental and emotional symbol become a part of your awareness, letting the energy flow all over you. Once you are done, draw the power symbol in front of you.

This meditation technique is usually done every day for at least a week. Take note of the changes that will transpire in your life during this period.

You can also use an alternative method of emotional healing by conducting a treatment. This treatment involves the use of all the hand positions as well as drawing of the mental and emotional symbol in each position. As you conduct the treatment, focus on the patterns or conditionings that are released, making use of your intuition.

CHAPTER 11

Reiki Distance Healing

Apart from hands-on healing, the Reiki system also works even if a practitioner or Reiki Master does not see, touch, or hear the client or recipient. Everyone may experience the Reiki healing through distance healing.

There are several distance healing methods used for sending Reiki energy. These methods do not necessarily use the distance healing symbol all the time. Once an individual becomes progressively familiar with the energy, he/she will be able to put aside the symbols; however, this may take time. One should be able to strengthen the connection to the energy.

It is likewise important to stay in the present state and be aware of one's actions when send distance healing. It is best not to attach one's self to the effect or result of the healing. Instead, one should simply send and allow the Reiki to do what is appropriate.

Methods for Reiki Distance Healing

Photo Technique

This method is regarded as the simplest way to send the Reiki to an individual at a distance using a photo of him/her. The method begins by drawing the three symbols of Reiki with the practitioner's finger on the client's or recipient's photo. Then, the names of each symbol are stated three times as the practitioner draws them. The practitioner's primary intention is to fill the individual with the Reiki. After which, the photo is placed between the hands of the practitioner to send the Reiki energy.

Some people also use this method for self treatment. The photo of the individual is simply placed under his/her hands, intending to receive the treatment.

Teddy Bear Method (Proxy Methods)

Proxy methods make use of objects or things that represent the client or recipient of the Reiki. These are used for developing harmony or gaining rapport with another individual. Given that most people find it difficult to believe that Reiki transcends space and time, these proxy methods provide them with a "guarantee" to grasp the concept of Reiki transcendence and overcome the limitations of their minds. In essence, the photo technique is also a proxy method, which makes use of a photo to represent a client or recipient. Consequently, a practitioner can use anything to serve as a proxy of the client or recipient.

In the teddy bear method, the assumption is to use a teddy bear as a proxy or representation of a client or recipient. It is easy to make intentions when using a teddy bear given that it has different parts that can represent the body parts of a client. For instance, its head can represent the head of the client and so on.

Proxy methods start by securing an object that represents the client and drawing the three symbols on it. The object should be treated just like treating the client in person.

Finger Method

This technique also makes use of a representation of the client or recipient when sending distance Reiki. It is often used when a practitioner is in a place where he/she intends to send distance Reiki without attracting attention to himself/herself. It is also useful when only one of the practitioner's hands is free.

The concept of the finger method is one of the fingers of a hand to represent a client or situation, which the practitioner wants to send distance Reiki to. The finger method begins by drawing the three symbols and wrapping the fingers of a hand around the finger, which the practitioner would use as a representation. The practitioner then intends to send distance Reiki to the client or situation. He/she can say the intention out loud. As the practitioner does the Reiki on his/her finger, the client or situation receives the distance Reiki as well.

Visualization Method

This technique involves the use of imagination. The practitioner imagines that he/she is with the client receiving the treatment. The practitioner does the healing as if he/she is with the client. The key in this method is to visualize the image of the client in the practitioner's mind while he/she does the Reiki. Thus, this method necessitates strong intent as well as visual skills.

Beaming Method

This method has two different techniques. Both beaming techniques "beam" or radiate the Reiki at a distance and in person radiating to an individual who is in the same location with the practitioner.

The beaming method begins by drawing the three symbols in the air and stating the client's name whom the practitioner intends to heal. The practitioner can also use other details about the client in which he/she feels more connected with. As the practitioner sends the Reiki energy, he/she intends that the client receives it as well. This is done by holding one or both hands about chest-high with palms facing outward from the practitioner. If only one hand is used, the other should be placed comfortably on the lap. Then, the practitioner sends the distance Reiki, feeling it radiate through his/her hands while the client receives the healing.

The in-person beaming method is also a type of distance Reiki; however, the practitioner is with the person whom he/she intends to heal. This method is useful if the practitioner wants to send the Reiki energy to an individual who is in his/her line of sight. It is also useful for persons with touch issues such as those who have infectious diseases, sexual traumas, or burn victims.

The in-person beaming method begins by extending the palms toward the client and using the word or symbol for distance healing. Unlike the typical distance healing, using the in-person beaming method entails seeing the client. A practitioner can also radiate the Reiki energy from his/her body or from the eyes, beaming out from every cell.

Distance Reiki on a List of Recipients

This technique involves doing the Reiki healing on a list of recipients with the intention that each of them would receive the Reiki treatment. Practitioners use this method when they have several people to treat at a distance but do not have the time to conduct distance healing for each individual.

This method begins by creating a list of the recipients that the practitioner intends to heal. The list may include the names, locations, ages, and situations of each recipient. It may also include the treatment required for each recipient. It is important that the practitioner has the permission of the recipients. Then, the list is empowered with the intention of filling it with the Reiki treatment for each recipient. Essentially, the practitioner is doing Reiki on the list. Then, he/she places his/her hands on the list to send the Reiki energy or simply visualize the recipients receiving the treatment. In general, distance healing takes about 15-20 minutes.

Creative Distance Healing

More often than not, practitioners have their own creative ways of doing the Reiki distance healing. Normally, it is used to send Reiki healing to an individual who is not close enough to be touched by a practitioner. Given that the Reiki distance healing transcends space and time, practitioners can also send it to the following:

one's self as a child, one's inner child, one's difficult situations in the past; global crises such as international terrorism, the Gulf war, etc.; one's self in the future, anticipating a difficult situation such as a job interview or public speaking; the Earth, nature, and one's own garden; one's past life or future life; another person who has passed on; divine figures and personalities such as Jesus Christ, the Goddess, the Buddha, Krishna, Jehovah, etc.; and healing a relationship for the "highest good" of two or more people.

Distance Healing Books

Many people may not believe it but one can send Reiki distance healing through books. A practitioner may simply write down the names of the recipients in a blank book, making sure to review the list prior to starting the treatment. The practitioner then channels the Reiki energy into the book intending that everyone in the book would receive the treatment.

This method of distance healing will work regardless if the practitioner does not know the client or recipient. It is said that there are healing "networks" that will serve as channels in sending the Reiki energy to the names given to them. While the recipient may not know the recipient, the latter who asked for the treatment knows the networks. Thus, such connection is enough for the Reiki energy to flow, fill, and heal the recipient.

Distance Healing Boxes

Some practitioners also make use of distance healing boxes to send the Reiki energy to recipients. These boxes contain pieces of paper wherein the names of the recipients are written. Others use the photographs of recipients. Practitioners simply do the Reiki to the box, intending to send the energy to each recipient represented in the box.

Doing the Reiki to a Bed

Another form of a creative distance healing is doing the Reiki to one's bed. For instance, one can send Reiki to his/her bed, intending for the energy to stay and wait for the individual. Once he/she lays on the bed, the Reiki energy will flow into him/her.

Group Distance Healing

This method of distance healing involves a number of practitioners or other Reiki healers who work together to heal other people. This is done either in person or at a distance. There are two common ways to do a group distance healing.

One, the practitioners or other Reiki healers sit together in a circle. Each participant of the group should face the back of the one in front of them. Then, each of them should draw the three symbols while connecting to the Reiki energy. The recipient's name, gender, age, location, and other details are stated. This is followed by sending the Reiki of each member of the healing group to the recipient.

Two, the practitioners or other Reiki healers sit together in a circle, this time, facing each other. As with the first technique, each member of the group draws the three symbols while connecting to the Reiki energy. The same details of the recipient are stated and everyone in the healing group then sends the Reiki energy to the recipient. However, all members of the healing group should be able to imagine or visualize the recipient being present in the middle of the circle.

CHAPTER 12

How to Disseminate Your Reiki Practice

Today, a great number of people is discovering Reiki as a wonderful gift for themselves and for their family and friends. This is the reason why many are encouraged to share or disseminate their Reiki practice in a broader scope.

An individual who decides to disseminate his or her Reiki practice can reap great rewards. Apart from having more meaningful spiritual experiences, disseminating Reiki practice can also provide one with a source of income.

Once an individual is initiated into Reiki, he or she already has the ability to impart Reiki healing energy to oneself and to others. Thus, an individual can already use several techniques to disseminate a Reiki practice.

Determining the Quality of Intention

When disseminating a Reiki practice, one of the most important factors to consider is the quality as well as the strength of one's intention. Given that the mind is similar to a magnet, it is necessary for you to maintain a positive mental perspective. This is because the quality and strength of your thoughts can discern what you attract into your life. Thus, during the dissemination of a Reiki practice, it is important to have a positive mental perspective.

When disseminating a Reiki practice, you should decide with commitment, determination, and clarity. You should decide your worthiness to disseminate a Reiki practice in which other people will benefit from your service. You should decide on the value that you and your clients will be receiving from your Reiki practice.

It will help if you try to visualize the outcome you want to achieve and how it would feel if you get involved actively in disseminating a Reiki practice. Meditating frequently can help visualize and feel the results you want. Allow the outcome to fill and surround you while reaching out to others.

You also need to be determined that a thriving Reiki practice is a valid objective, which you are trying to establish. Know that it will give you satisfaction, freedom, and joy. In other words, you have to believe in yourself as well as your purpose in disseminating a Reiki practice.

In case you have doubts about your goals, try not to panic. It is normal for doubts to arise; however, you just have to let them pass and remove them out of your consciousness. As you commit to your new goal or level of healing, the negative feelings and thoughts stored inside you are discarded, especially if you have a strong commitment to your new goal. As a matter of fact, negative thoughts and feelings that arise are part of your healing and you will become healed as you release them to the Higher Power. To speed up the process of your healing, you can use your Reiki.

Calling on Higher Sources of Help

There are higher sources that you can call on for help when disseminating a Reiki practice. These include Reiki spirit guides, beings of light, and angels. You can also call on your enlightened self to help you in developing your Reiki practice. For instance, you can call upon these higher sources to direct clients to you as well as assist you during treatment sessions.

While these higher sources are available, you need to have a strong spiritual intention for them to work. If you have a selfish intention in doing Reiki, such as gaining control over others, taking extra air of self-importance, or doing Reiki only for money, it would be hard for the higher sources to help you.

There should be an alignment or congruity within you so that the Higher Power of Reiki will flow through you in a significant way. Consequently, if there is alignment and purity of intentions, higher sources and other spiritual beings will work with you.

Reiki only wants what is best for any individual using it; however, the individual should align with Reiki's nature to receive the greatest benefits. An individual who has an unselfish heart and a desire to help others can open more to Reiki's true nature. In turn, the spirit of Reiki will provide even more guidance.

If you want to have a successful Reiki practice, it is best to focus on healing and helping others with love and compassion.

Fear of Competition Contradicts the Nature of Reiki

One of the most common factors that can hinder in developing a spiritual orientation about a Reiki practice is having the fear of competition. This is because it can cause added negative energy as well as restrictions in the community of Reiki. As compared to the Reiki practitioners available, there is a greater need for healing in this world. If there is fear of competition, it can drive back people who may be interested in experiencing a Reiki treatment from you.

Reiki does not fear competition given that it is from an unlimited supply of positive energy. Individuals who do Reiki together get stronger, especially if there are more people who join the group. If Reiki becomes competitive, people in the group get weaker. Moreover, if Reiki is competitive, instead of having other people do the Reiki with you, you will alone. Competitiveness in Reiki results in the exact opposite of the system's purpose.

The Reiki energy's nature is based on cooperation. This entails that people are one and that the energy can flow to anyone and everyone freely. The Reiki only works if there is harmony. The wisdom of Reiki is to recognize and accept all other practitioners as allies rather than competitors.

If you have a spiritual purpose of a Reiki practice to heal the world and help other people, then hearing about another Reiki practitioner in your vicinity should bring you gladness because he or she can help in fulfilling your purpose.

Once you accept the wisdom of Reiki as yours, you will learn to accept that other people who also practice the Reiki are helping you in your purpose. The more you do this, the more you will thrive in your Reiki practice.

You might be worrying about other practitioners taking away your clients from you. But just keep in mind that that every practitioner has their own special way and value to help others. In addition, you will only attract the clients who are appropriate for your own value as a practitioner. In the same manner, other practitioners will only attract clients who are appropriate for their own value.

Keeping Reiki Free from Government Regulation

Nowadays, the general public is increasingly recognizing the value of Reiki as a complementary or alternative method of healing. As a matter of fact, Reiki is becoming more popular through word of mouth in which people who have experienced it attest to its efficiency and great ability to heal. The increase in the use of Reiki both by independent practitioners and in clinics and hospitals is caused by Reiki's undeniable effectiveness.

As Reiki is being used in thousands of hospitals across the globe, it results in bringing up the question of government regulation. Some people and groups have thought of Reiki as just another type of medical practice, which should be licensed and regulated.

In most states of the United States of America, the current medical practice act considers Reiki as a medical practice; thus, it requires that only licensed health care providers should carry out Reiki treatments. On the other hand, although this law or act currently exists, it is rarely enforced. However, since this law exists, all Reiki practitioners are placed under unnecessary threat.

The only purpose of this law is protecting the public from harm; however, Reiki does not cause any harm at all, which is why there should not be any law requiring practitioners, teachers, or Reiki Masters to get licenses. Any Reiki practice should be free from government regulation given that it is not harmful to the public.

Practical Ways to Disseminate Your Reiki Practice

Money Issues

Once you have the right attitude, belief, and value needed for disseminating your Reiki practice, it is likewise important to deal with the issue of money. There are a number of Reiki practitioners who do not charge money from their customers. It is up to the practitioner whether or not he/she will charge the clients. On the other hand, most clients feel better if they are able to compensate the services of their Reiki practitioners.

It is just right to take note that when clients choose to pay for your Reiki services, it is not the Reiki energy that they are paying for; but, your effort and time spent in learning Reiki. More often than not, clients who receive Reiki treatment for free feel indebted as well as guilty. As such, it develops an imbalance, which can hinder proper treatment. Charging money is often a better alternative for clients as they feel free to come to you to receive the Reiki any time they want. In case some of your clients have financial problems, you can charge them less.

In general, the charge for a Reiki session depends on the area where you do your Reiki practice. It is best to charge the same fee as other Reiki practitioners in your area. The standard Reiki treatment session usually lasts about 45 minutes to 1 ½ hours. If you are just starting with your Reiki practice, it is advisable to start with a lower rate. You can just increase it as your reputation grows.

Advertising a Reiki Practice

There are several ways to advertise your Reiki practice. These include business cards and flyers. Business cards let clients know that you are dedicated about your Reiki. They also bear your contact number in case the clients want to schedule an appointment. When making your business card, it is best exclude your address to avoid coming to your place without calling for an appointment. It is advisable to talk to your clients first so that you will get a feel for energy and let them become aware of what they can expect from your Reiki treatment prior to having an appointment. Once you have talked to your clients, you can already provide them your address in case you are interested for a Reiki session.

Flyers are also one way to advertise your Reiki practice. When creating your flyer, make sure to explain the concept of Reiki along with the benefits it can offer clients. Your flyer should also include your name and contact number. It is advisable to place flyers in health food stores, book stores, and/or other places where you can distribute them to clients.

If you are starting with disseminating your Reiki practice, it is advisable to start from your home first so that it can save money. However, most practitioners find it more advantageous to have their own Reiki office than have sessions at home. They claim that an office has a professional ambiance, letting clients know that they are taking their work seriously. If you can afford to rent or establish an office, you may do so. However, if you want to avoid start-up expenses, you can do your Reiki practice at home.

Take note that in a Reiki practice, you may involve group activities; as such, you should consider the size of the area in which you will conduct your sessions.

Once you have clients, make sure you secure their name, address, and contact number to include them in your mailing list. You can mail your flyers about your Reiki practice and events.

Exchanging Reiki Practice with Other Providers of Alternative Therapy

One effective way to disseminate your Reiki practice is offering an exchange with other alternative therapists. For instance, you can call on massage therapists who are efficient with body work and likewise need to have Reiki therapy themselves. You can offer a Reiki session to these therapists and let them refer you to their clients. Provide them with your business cards or ask them to display your flyers in their offices.

Providing Impromptu Reiki Sessions

You can disseminate your Reiki practice effectively when you offer it to people who complain about pain or aches in public gatherings. For instance, if you are in a meeting or even a party and someone complains of a body pain, you can offer the individual a Reiki treatment. You can also offer to reduce their stress along with other health benefits.

Start by talking to them in a way that they can easily understand the concept of the Reiki system. It would take about 15 minutes or so to address and threat their concern. Let them know that you are doing the Reiki practice professionally and provide them with your business card. You can tell your prospective clients about the inclusions of a complete Reiki session and encourage them to set an appointment if interested.

During public gatherings, especially large ones, you are most likely to attract a number of people when you give one individual a Reiki treatment. You can do this to provide a sample of how your Reiki practice works. More often than not, you would probably have sessions for several people, giving them your business cards in the end.

While treating people in public gatherings, you can talk about your Reiki practice, its benefits, and how it can work for them. You may also ask them to explain or share how they feel and provide them information as to how Reiki can help them.

One of the key factors to attracting people in your Reiki practice is being focused on healing them instead of getting them as a client. If they are interested, on the other hand, you can always hand them your business card.

In public gatherings, you can also wear a Reiki shirt, including its symbols. Most likely, people will become curious about what the symbols are, giving you the chance to talk about the Reiki. You can then offer them a sample session while telling them that you do it professionally. Once people get interested, you can hand them your business card and set an appointment.

Offering Free Monthly Reiki Sample Treatments

Planning one night every month to conduct a Reiki session free of charge can help in disseminating your practice. Many people will become interested if you offer them free Reiki session once a month. You can send out flyers for your free evening Reiki session or place them in public areas. This is a remarkable way of helping others learn about the Reiki as well as your practice. During this once-a-month session, you can provide clients your business card so they can contact you if they want to have an appointment.

It would even help if you have Reiki friends who can help you in giving treatments to potential or interested clients. It is advisable to meet up with other Reiki practitioners who can help you an hour or so prior to giving treatments to other people. This will improve the quality of the Reiki that you can provide potential clients. This is a powerful healing experience while demonstrating the benefits of Reiki to other people.

If you have taken the training for Reiki Masters or the third level training, you can provide other practitioners with a healing or refresher attunement in order to boost their Reiki energy. It is also an excellent way for practitioners to practice Reiki. In turn you can also practice providing attunements.

You may call people you know who may be interested in receiving Reiki. You can also get a booth if your vicinity offers holistic or psychic fairs. For instance, you can take a Reiki table with your Reiki friends who can help you in the treatments. Offer interested people a 10- or 15-minute session while your Reiki friends give treatments to another person at a time. You and the other practitioners can also use chairs while treating people. Chairs take up lesser space than tables. Make sure you bring your business cards and flyers with you and get each individual's name, contact number, and address for your mailing list.

Offering Reiki as a Means of Public Service

A great way for people to create interest in the Reiki system is offering it as a means of public service. You can do this during a healing service at the church. You can volunteer to conduct free Reiki treatments in hospice centers, hospitals, and drug/alcohol treatment centers. You can also offer free Reiki service together with a psychologist or other practitioners. Apart from people finding out about your Reiki practice, you also gain experience while helping others.

Writing Articles About Reiki Healing

If you have the chance to write articles about Reiki, say, in the community, holistic or metaphysical paper in your area, do so. It is best if you can write articles about Reiki healing at least every month. Make sure you include your name and contact number in the article. In addition, you should also mention that you are a Reiki teacher or practitioner and let people know about your beliefs and attitudes associated with Reiki healing. You can also place an ad in the paper where you write articles. While you may be charged for the ad, your article is free. Furthermore, when writing your articles, include recent news about Reiki and provide stories about your Reiki experiences both in receiving it and during treatments.

Conducting Talks About Reiki

If you have connections with local groups, you can conduct a Reiki talk for free. There are various groups that are seeking for speakers who can provide talks about alternative healing. It would be an advantage if you have an experience in public speaking; however, you need not be an expert public speaker to talk about the Reiki system. On the other hand, if you are planning to make your Reiki practice a career, you need to ability to speak before groups of people.

Using the Media

You can maximize the local media in your area as most of them are interested in reporting about different types of alternative healing. You may approach radio and television stations as well as local newspapers to disseminate your Reiki practice. Make sure you know the reporters who are responsible for reporting news about alternative healing. Speak to them and let provide them awareness about the Reiki system. Also, make sure you let them know that you are a Reiki teacher or practitioner. This way, they will become more interested in seeking news from you given that you have the credibility to provide pertinent information. You can talk to the press in a way that they will easily understand your purpose as well as the benefits of your Reiki practice.

CHAPTER 13

Frequently Asked Questions About Reiki

There are several questions that are commonly asked about Reiki. In this chapter, these questions will be answered to help individuals get a clear and accurate knowledge about the Reiki system.

Where does the Reiki energy originate?

Reiki energy is usually perceived as a subtle energy, which is different from other physical energy, such as chemical energy or electricity. Reiki energy originates from the Higher Power. The Higher Power is found on a dimension, which is higher than the physical world that people have come to know.

When the Reiki energy is perceived in a precognitive manner, it may seem to come down from up above, entering the top of a Reiki practitioner's head. Then, it may appear to flow through the practitioner's body and coming out of the hands. On the other hand, the real source of the Reiki energy is within oneself. The energy comes from a transcendental part of oneself, which is linked to an inexhaustible healing energy supply.

Is the Reiki system a type of religion?

While Reiki is fundamentally spiritual, it is not considered a religion. For one, the Reiki system does not demand practitioners to change their spiritual or religious beliefs. Practitioners have the freedom to preserve what they believe in and make decisions based on the nature of their religious beliefs and practices.

How is a Reiki treatment administered?

In a basic treatment, the Reiki energy flows from a practitioner's hands going to the client. More often than not, the client is lying on a massage table; however, Reiki treatments can also be administered even if the client prefers to stand or sit.

During the treatment, the client is fully clothed. The practitioner directs his or her hands on the client's body, making use of various hand positions. The practitioner usually places his or her hands around the head, stomach, shoulders, and feet of the client. The practitioner can also use more specific positions depending on the needs of the client.

Each position is held for at least 3 to 10 minutes. Once again, this depends on how much flow of Reiki energy the client needs. A standard treatment usually takes 45 minutes to 1 ½ hours.

How does a Reiki treatment feel?

The experience or feeling during a Reiki treatment is different from one client to another. However, all clients of a Reiki treatment will definitely experience a feeling of deep relaxation. In most cases, clients tend to drift off to sleep during the treatment.

Most clients who have already experienced a Reiki treatment claimed to have a glowing radiance surrounding and flowing through them. In addition, a state of well-being and peace is experienced given that the Reiki energy promotes letting go of all fear, anxiety, tension, or other negative feelings. Others claim to float outside their bodies while some claim to have mystical visions or experiences.

Once the treatment session ends, a client would surely feel refreshed and at the same time have a more balanced and positive outlook.

What does Reiki treat?

Reiki has a positive effect on almost all kinds of negative conditions and illness. These include minor physical conditions, such as bee stings, stomach aches, flu, and colds and major physical conditions, such as cancer, heart disease, and leukemia among others. Reiki also has the ability to relieve emotional and mental problems, including anxiety and depression.

Reiki can also reduce or eliminate side effects from regular medical treatments, including post-operative depression and pain and negative effects of chemotherapy. It can also improve one's healing rate as well as reduce the period of hospital confinement.

There are numerous cases wherein Reiki treatment has helped. In fact, some people who have gone through Reiki treatment sessions have claimed complete healing as confirmed from their medical tests before and after they have undergone Reiki treatment.

While Reiki can bring about miracles to some clients, this cannot be vouched. The true promise of a Reiki treatment is reduction of stress as well as improvement in an individual's psychological and physical condition.

To receive a Reiki treatment, does one need to stop seeing a psychologist or regular doctor?

An individual who wants to experience a Reiki treatment does not need to stop seeing his or her doctor. This is because Reiki can work in conjunction with regular psychological or medical treatments.

In fact, most Reiki practitioners would recommend seeing a licensed health care specialist in addition to undergoing Reiki treatment sessions, especially if the client has a psychological or medical condition.

Reiki can work with all other healing forms, including surgery, medications, alternative care methods, and psychological care.

Can anyone learn to do the Reiki?

Given that Reiki is a simple technique, more and more people regardless of age, gender, or nationality, are learning it. One does not need any prior experience with meditation, healing, or any type of training to learn the Reiki. This is because it is taught in a non-conventional manner where a teacher transfers the Reiki energy to the student through a process referred to as attunement. Once the student receives an attunement, he or she already has the ability to do the Reiki. The student can already place his or her hands to treat oneself or another individual as the healing Reiki energy automatically begins to flow.

Are children allowed to learn the Reiki?

Even children can learn the Reiki as long as they are old enough to understand the concepts of the Reiki system. It is also recommended for children to receive the Reiki.

How many levels are there in a Reiki training?

There are four levels in a Reiki training based on the Usui or Tibetan Reiki system. These include first, second, advanced, and Master levels.

How long will it take for one to learn the Reiki?

More often than not, Reiki centers that offer classes start on a weekend, specifically for beginners. The class usually takes one or two days. It is highly recommended to finish at least 6 to seven hours of a Reiki class. In addition, apart from the attunement, a student is also shown how to give treatments to oneself and to others as well as practice giving treatments during class.

What does Reiki attunement mean?

A Reiki attunement is the process wherein an individual receives the ability to provide Reiki treatments. During a Reiki class, a Reiki Master administers the attunement and touches the head, shoulders, and hands of the student while making use of one or more breathing techniques. The attunement energies then flow through the Reiki Master going to the student. Attunement energies are special energies, which are guided by the Higher Power. These energies also adjust through the energy pathways of the student, connecting him or her to the Reiki source.

During the attunement, the energetic aspect, which is guided by the Higher Power adjusts itself to become exactly what the student needs. Some students may have visions of spiritual beings or see colors during the attunement. Others may feel warmth in their hands. On the other hand, students undergoing an attunement may simply feel more relaxed without having an inner experience. In both cases, an attunement works.

Can an individual get more than one attunement?

An attunement lasts a lifetime; as such, when one receives as attunement, it will last his or her whole life. If one gets an additional attunement for the similar level, it will strengthen and refine the Reiki energy.

What is lineage?

Once an individual receives Reiki, he or she will be part of a succession of teachers, which leads to the founder of the Reiki system. For instance, if a teacher practices the Usui Reiki, the lineage would lead to Dr. Usui.

What can an individual expect or feel when giving a Reiki treatment?

When a practitioner gives a Reiki treatment, the Reiki energy flows through him or her prior to leaving the hands and flowing to the client. As such, the practitioner also receives a treatment. When the Reiki energy flows, the practitioner will feel uplifted and more relaxed. Some practitioners claim to have spiritual experiences when giving treatment. Others claim to receive insights about the client's needs, allowing them to heal in a deeper way.

Can a practitioner treat oneself?

Once a practitioner receives the attunement, he or she can treat oneself and others. This is one of Reiki's unique features as other types of healing or treatment do not allow an individual to treat oneself.

How does sending Reiki to others at a distance work?

During the second level of the Reiki training, a practitioner is given three symbols, which are empowered during the attunement. One of the three symbols include distant healing.

Reiki distance healing works by securing a picture of the individual whom the practitioner wants to send Reiki to. The practitioner may also write the individual's name on a paper; think of the person; or activate the distant symbol to send Reiki regardless of where the individual is located. There is no difference in the quality of Reiki healing a practitioner provides whether the client is near or hundreds of miles away. The Reiki energy will go directly to the client and treat him or her. Some practitioners also send Reiki to world leaders, especially during critical or crisis situations to help them.

Is Reiki treatment safe for pregnant women?

Given that the Reiki energy is guided by the Higher Power, it will know the client's condition and adjust as needed. Only positive and good things are provided during a Reiki treatment. As such, many women, even those who are pregnant receive Reiki treatments. Apart from providing great benefits to pregnant women, Reiki also treats the unborn child. Reiki is also used during child birth.

Is Reiki treatment safe for babies?

As mentioned previously, Reiki can only result in good things. Most babies who have received Reiki treatment love it. The Reiki energy adjusts to the needs of babies; therefore, parents do not need to worry about the treatment or energy being too strong.

Can Reiki also treat animals and plants?

Most animals that receive Reiki treatment seem to have an innate understanding of the Reiki as well as its benefits. Plants also have a positive response to Reiki as they grow healthier and stronger.

Does the Reiki treatment involve any side effects?

While people who receive the Reiki treatment feel uplifted and relaxed after a Reiki treatment, some individuals experience a "healing crisis." When an individual's vibration heightens, the toxins stored in the body are released into the blood stream, filtered by the kidneys and liver, and removed from the system. As a result, an individual may feel weak, or experience a stomach ache, or a headache. More often than not, practitioners recommend that the client experiencing these minor side effects drink more water, get more rest, and eat lighter meals. A huge part of the Reiki treatment is cleansing the body.

Can Reiki help groups of people during global crises?

One of the unique benefits of Reiki is that it is able encourage groups of people to do positive things even during challenging global situations. It is able to reduce the suffering of people across the globe.

How can an individual find a Reiki teacher who is right for him or her?

More often than not, Reiki Masters, practitioners, or teachers post advertisements in magazines, health food stores, book stores, and other places. When an individual finds a Reiki teacher, it is advisable to ask important questions to help in determining whether the said teacher is a good choice.

Some of the common questions to ask Reiki Masters, practitioners, or teachers include: how long have they been working with Reiki; what training have they undergone; how do they use Reiki personally; what is their lineage; how often do they teaches Reiki; what is covered in their classes; what qualifications are required in their Reiki training; how many hours of class time do they include; how much time is hands-on practice and instructional; what are their fees; does the class include a manual and certificate; and are they open to supporting students to become successful Reiki teachers or practitioners among others.

An individual should be aware of his or her feelings about the answers to his or her questions. A Reiki Master should be able to respond in a supportive, loving, and empowering manner. The individual should listen to his or her heart as the Reiki Master answers the questions.

How much is cost for each Reiki treatment?

A Reiki treatment generally costs around $25 to $100. The rate depends on the area as well as the country. On the other hand, some practitioners offer Reiki treatments for a donation or even free of charge.

Can an individual make Reiki a source of income?

If an individual puts his or her heart into Reiki, he or she can develop a Reiki practice while conducting classes. This is a fulfilling way that result in regular income.

Can an individual become "licensed" to practice and teach Reiki?

As of now, there are no licensing programs that any government provides to become a "licensed" Reiki practitioner. However, there are some Reiki centers that offer licensing programs for Reiki teachers.

Are Reiki treatments covered by insurance?

Some insurance companies cover Reiki treatments although most of them are just starting to recognize Reiki.

CHAPTER 14

Success Stories About Reiki Healing

People who have experienced the Reiki healing have various success stories, which they have testified about. These stories range from physical to emotional problems to psychological to spiritual issues. This chapter is about real stories of people who have experienced the Reiki healing and made them a whole new individual with good health and a positive disposition in life.

Healed Heart Problem (Kay Peters, Jefferson County)

In 2000, Kay felt ill and decided to carry out a number of physical tests from a health care professional. It turned out that she had a silent heart attack as well as diabetes. Her doctor even told her that she needs to undergo a heart catheterization; thus, she immediately have the procedure scheduled.

Kay lived in the rural region; however, she needed to travel to New York for her work. While waiting for two weeks for her scheduled heart catheterization, Kay met a woman during a college graduation party of a friend. The woman asked her if she was feeling fine. Then, the woman offered Kay to come to her house within the week. Kay can only go to the woman's house a night prior to travelling four hours to New York for her scheduled medical procedure. Still, she decided to go to the woman's house.

Upon her arrival, the woman asked her if she have heard about the Reiki, which she had not. The woman asked her if she can do a treatment for Kay. Thinking that she had nothing to lose, Kay went for the treatment.

An hour later, Kay felt wonderful after the Reiki treatment. She became extremely calm yet emotional, which relieved her. When the woman was done with the treatment, Kay got to know a lot about the Reiki. She felt so different, protected, and loved after experiencing the Reiki treatment.

The next day, she went for the procedure, which made her scared. In fact, during the procedure, she cried as fear took over her. The doctor told Kay to look at the monitors, telling her that her heart was healthy based on the screens. Furthermore, there was no evidence that Kay had a heart attack. The only issue she had was a small valve problem.

After the procedure, the doctor came to Kay's room saying that based on the 2d-echo, ultrasound, and other tests conducted prior to the procedure, he was sure that Kay had a heart attack. All the tests indicated that a heart attack took place; however, when the scheduled medical procedure came, no evidence was seen on the monitors. The doctor did not understand what transpired; but Kay did.

When Kay got home the next day, she called the woman, her Reiki teacher and told her what happened in the hospital. Thus, Kay became eager to know more about Reiki healing and decided to learn and use it. Today, Kay is already a Reiki Master.

Healed Severe Infection (Kathleen Bailey, Hudson, New Jersey)

Kathleen, a Reiki practitioner, had a friend named Marie who was brought to the hospital for reconstructive surgery caused by breast cancer. A few weeks after the surgery, Kathleen met Marie's husband and asked about her health. The couple was devastated as Marie developed a severe infection. Marie had fever of 104 degrees for a few days. The doctors were not able to detect where the infection came from. Marie's husband said that the doctors believed her organs would start to shut down.

Kathleen then asked permission from Marie's husband to visit her. The couple agreed and Kathleen began sending the Reiki to Marie. The next morning after the treatment, Marie said she felt well and even looked great. Kathleen asked Marie how she felt and the latter said her temperature was already normal. Her doctors were not able to explain her healing.

Then, Marie asked Kathleen what the Reiki is. Kathleen decided to put her hands over the area where Marie had her severe infection. Kathleen closed her eyes and began sending the Reiki again to Marie.

Marie is now recuperating in their home with her family. She continues to see Kathleen for Reiki healing.

Prostate Cancer Gone (Fran Gacher, Lawrence, Kansas)

Fran Gacher heard of Reiki from a friend, but was skeptical to try it. He then called an assisted-living center that offers free mini-Reiki sessions as well as classes for Introduction to Reiki. Fran asked the social director how familiar he was with the Reiki. The social director told Fran that he was recently diagnosed with prostate cancer. A Reiki Level II therapist told him (the social director) that it is necessary for him to receive three Reiki treatments in close succession with three Reiki healers. The social director decided to go for the treatments. He only received the Reiki and refused to undergo an medical tests and procedures. He did not even take medicines.

Before the Reiki treatment, the social director's test results showed that his prostate cancer cells have increased to 4.0. After the Reiki treatment, the social director was tested again by his doctor. Results showed that he only had 0.3 and that he was cancer-free. The doctor even said that the test results were the lowest he had ever encountered. The social director felt that the Reiki had become a major part of his life and until now, he still undergoes Reiki sessions for continued good health.

Healed Malignant Uterus (Margaret Levy, Whittier, Los Angeles)

Margaret's officemate, Denise was diagnosed with a tumor in her uterus. Doctors took her blood samples and carried out ultrasounds and biopsies, which all indicated that Denise had malignancy in her uterus. She was only 21 years old with five-year old twin daughters. Apart from working full time and being a mother to her children, she was also completing a diploma in youth counseling and four certificates in tourism.

Margaret, a Reiki practitioner, gave her friend two short Reiki treatments. Every night, Margaret also sent Denise the Reiki while asking other Reiki friends to pray for her and heal her. Margaret and her Reiki friends continued to heal Denise for a month prior to undergoing the surgery to remove the tumor.

Before the scheduled surgery, Denise went for a pre-operation consultation. The doctors were surprised to find out that the tumor was gone. To be extremely sure, the doctors did all the tests again and only found a little of scar tissue from the tumor's area. There were also no signs of the tumor in Denise's blood.

Back Injuries and Depression Cured (Kemp Carson, Moraga, San Francisco)

In 1980, Kemp had a serious accident at work, which caused a number of problems in his back such as pinched nerves, stretched muscles, arthritis, and herniated discs among others. He tried to go to several chiropractors, take pain killers, and other ways to relieve his back problems.

Twelve years after, Kemp met another accident where he slipped and fell on ice while he was about to leave work. This caused more pain and herniations to his back and a broken arm. In addition, it was another traumatic experience. He spent almost 2 years in bed, taking a number of medicines to numb his pain. This experience also left Kemp in a mess with depression.

When Kemp decided to attend his high school reunion, he met her friend, Shirley who urged him to receive a Reiki treatment. Shirley told him that she was also receiving Reiki treatments for her depression.

Given that Kemp was already desperate to get rid of the pain and his medicines, he took the Reiki treatment and attended classes with Shirley. Immediately after his first treatment, Kemp's strength got back, his energy was changed into a positive one, and his depression was lifted. All his negative feelings gone in just a few sessions that followed.

Today, Kemp is still recuperating from the accidents slowly; however, he can already walk and swim. He is also taking arthritis aqua class and walks on a treadmill. Doctors said that he could no longer walk after the second accident. However, he is able to walk now that he continues to receive the Reiki and take classes. He is now on Reiki II and plans to take the Reiki Master level to heal both himself and others who need the Reiki.

Abscessed Tooth Saved (Peter Hamilton, Fremont, New Hampshire)

Peter complained of having a severe toothache for 2 nights and decided to see his dentist. He was told that he had an abscessed tooth and needed to undergo a root canal and crown. However, he failed to sign up for a dental insurance in his work. He could not afford the dental procedures. Peter asked his wife, Sandra, a Reiki practitioner, to do the Reiki healing on his tooth or the side of his face. Prior to this, Peter did not believe Sandra about what Reiki can do.

After a treatment, Peter felt relieved and had his dental appointment cancelled. The dentist insisted to see Peter. The latter undergone an x-ray and the dentist no longer saw the infection in Peter's tooth.

Although there may be little twinges of Peter's tooth every now and then, he did not have problems about dealing with the pain as he continued to receive the Reiki healing from his wife, Sandra.

Stroke Healed (George Peyton, Alberta, Canada)

George Peyton was 80 years old when he suffered a stroke. He had difficulty walking because he lost his balance. He also had mild weakness on the entire left side of his body. George also had double vision, which often caused him to become dizzy. He fell most of the time when he tried to walk his house; thus, his wife would not allow him to walk outdoors. Furthermore, George felt like there were worms crawling inside his head. He decided to see a neuro surgeon, neurologist, and even a balance therapist. However, there was no improvement in his condition. Worse, he started vomiting as an indication of more awful symptoms.

George heard a friend about the Reiki healing and its health benefits. He learned that Reiki can make him well complemented with cranialsacreal therapy and balancing exercises. He decided to join a Reiki treatment session in his area. After attending only four treatment sessions, the 80-year old man completely recovered.

Now, apart from going for long walks without complaints, George can already drive. He no longer had problems about double vision and dizziness. He also did not feel anything in his head anymore. It was like he regained his youthful energy.

Every treatment, George always went into deep relaxation for about 30 seconds. He felt heavenly and attested that Reiki can indeed result in miracles.

Healing Sick Pets (Gwen Carter, Richfield, Minnesota)

Gwen and her youngest daughter Cary share Reiki with those around them. Cary became interested in Reiki because Gwen does it in front of her. Cary often observed how her mother was able to treat other people through the Reiki energy. This was why Cary requested Gwen to provide her books about the Reiki. When Cary turned 11 years old, she received the Level II attunement. Together with Gwen, both of them integrated the Reiki system in all aspects of their lives.

One night, Gwen and Cary found an injured cat and decided to bring it to the veterinary clinic. The doctor said that the cat lost most of its left ear with an open wound on its right ear, about 2 ½ inches wide. Fortunately, the cat did not have any infection so the wounds were just treated and Gwen and Cary brought it home with them.

The mother and daughter named their new-found cat, Miracle. Miracle was obviously happy because of the attention given to her. It was also responsive. After a couple of days, Gwen decided to give a 10-minute Reiki session to Miracle for continued healing. The next day, the exposed tissue found on the cat's right ear turned from dark red to light pink. This made both Gwen and Cary glad, which was why they spent a few minutes every day to do the Reiki on Miracle to intensify its healing. After a total of twelve hours of short Reiki sessions, the healing of Miracle was already visible. The cat's right ear healed completely and its strength was already 100%.

No More Hearing Problems (Marsha Mitchell, Santa Clara County, San Jose)

Marsha was a Level II practitioner while her husband, Tony was a Level 1 practitioner. They offered a neighbor to provide her with a Reiki treatment in exchange for looking out for their two dogs. Prior to the Reiki treatment, their neighbor kept on asking them to do something about her shoulder. Both Marsha and her husband made no promises. They just told their neighbor that she will receive the treatment and feel more relaxed.

When the day of the treatment arrived, Marsha's neighbor kept pointing to her shoulder as the most affected part of her body. However, Tony kept working on her neck and head. Tony felt guided to those specific spots although he also treated the shoulder of their neighbor.

After the treatment, Marsha's neighbor showed a quizzical look on her face. She asked Marsha to whisper anything to her left ear. Marsha did not understand but went ahead to whisper something that made little sense. Marsha saw that her neighbor's eyes became wide while repeating what Marsha whispered to her. It was then that Marsha and Tony found out that their neighbor's left ear was clinically deaf since she was four years old.

Although their neighbor's shoulders still feels a little uneasy, she can already hear clearly as a bat.

Detected Mass (Arthur Hart, Philadelphia)

Arthur is a Reiki practitioner. His friend, Matthew was skeptical about the Reiki, telling Arthur to do the Reiki to him, whatever it is. Arthur decided to scan the body of Matthew using the Reiki energy. He was specifically drawn to Matthew's chest area, particularly the areola. Arthur's hands instantly turned to ice when he touched the areola of Matthew. Arthur could not describe what he felt and no matter how he ignored it, the Reiki energy drives him back to that area. When Arthur decided to stop but his hands felt like ice. Matthew also felt the hands of Arthur and got stunned. Then, Arthur decided to continue the treatment and began assessing Matthew's areola. To his surprise, he felt a huge mass in Matthew's chest wall.

Matthew felt the cold hands of Arthur who dragged him to see a doctor. The surgeon said that Matthew needed to undergo a surgery immediately to remove the huge mass. If Matthew refused the surgery, the mass would put pressure on his heart, which can cause death.

It was Arthur's first time to experience that Reiki can also detect lumps and masses in one's body. Until now, he is still amazed on how he was able to detect his friend's mass, which nearly caused his death. Arthur is now on Level II and plans to take the Reiki Master attunement to continue healing other people.

Healed Cancerous Tumor (Marlene Duerson, Winnipeg, Canada)

Marlene Duerson is a Master Reiki who encountered a client with a dilated lower abdomen. The client was sick for a number of months. The doctor told him that his x-ray revealed a cancerous tumor in his abdomen. He was then scheduled to have a medical procedure the following week.

Prior to the medical procedure, Marlene conducted a three-hour Reiki sessions for a week. When the client was about to be admitted to the hospital, Marlene saw a large black ball with sparkling light lift from her client's abdomen. The ball rose up into the area, disappearing through the ceiling. The other Reiki practitioners who were with Marlene also saw the black ball.

After the client was admitted to the hospital, the doctors examined him and ran tests. They were surprised to find out that the tumor was gone. They conducted another x-ray and found nothing. Given that it was unbelievable for the tumor to be gone, the doctors did an exploratory surgery. Amazed, they found no tumor in the client's abdomen.

The client underwent chemotherapy as a precaution for the possibility of some other types of cancer cells to develop. However, this cannot change the fact that the Reiki treatment sessions that the client received took away the cancerous tumor from him.

Healed Meningitis (Barbara Powell, San Ramon, San Francisco)

Barbara Powell is a mother of a seven-year old girl who suddenly became ill with the symptoms of meningitis. Barbara heard about a Reiki training center in her area and decided to send a healing request for her daughter. The little girl's brain swelled, making her unconscious. She was then rushed to the hospital and placed on a life-support system.

Barbara was devastated along with her husband. Their doctor were suspected with a damaged brain even if she regained consciousness. The doctor also warned the parents that the little girl may not be able to breathe on her own. At some point, they were told that they should decide to turn off the life support system and let go of their daughter.

However, after Barbara sent the healing request, her daughter's condition improved. In fact, the life support system was taken off and she was already permitted to go home. Barbara's daughter can already talk, sing, and even dance. She was able to attend her school. Barbara continued to send healing requests to the Reiki training center while her daughter also does physiotherapy for one leg.

Tumor Disappeared (Marlon Bradford, Minneapolis)

Marlon Bradford had a girlfriend, Linda, who experienced great pain in her right kidney area. Her doctor said that she had kidney stones although she can wait for them to be removed. When the doctor performed further tests on Linda, they showed a tumor on her kidney's right side, which was about the size of a regular egg. The doctor told Linda that the tumor should be closely examined through a cystoscope.

Marlon and Linda decided to schedule a cystoscope procedure a week after she was diagnosed. Marlon said that his girlfriend was in excruciating pain even after the doctor already gave her pain relievers. At first, the pain was relieved; however, it worsened until the pills could no longer ease the pain.

Marlon asked his Reiki friend to help his girlfriend, Linda. Marlon's Reiki friend immediately sent Reiki to Linda and offered to continue healing her until her scheduled cystoscope procedure. Each time Linda woke up in the morning, she felt relieved and no longer felt pain.

After a week, Linda underwent the scheduled procedure. Her doctor said that the tumor was gone. He asked Linda to go to a more experienced doctor to make sure that the tumor was totally eliminated. Marlon and Linda went to another doctor and the latter found the same results. The tumor was gone and her bladder was free from any kind of infection.

Conclusion

Thank you again for purchasing this book!

I hope this book was able to help you to learn and understand the concept of Reiki healing.

Through this book, you have now ventured into a journey of learning and discovery of the Reiki system of natural healing. However, it is up to you have far you can take the Reiki into your life. You have the option of undergoing through all the Reiki levels or simply stop on the first one. Whatever your decision may be, you should keep in mind that you do it because it is the most appropriate option for you.

Once you receive a Reiki attunement, you can already practice Reiki healing on yourself as well as to your family, friends, and even animals. However, know that you still cannot teach the Reiki unless you are already attuned to the Master level.

The most important part of the Reiki system is being able to heal while enjoying it. When you are already attuned, it is expected for your body to go through a process of adaptation. There are various ways in which this adaptation process can manifest. You may experience cold, headaches, or spots among others. However, these are only short-lived. You can focus on self treatments during the adaptation process, intending to enhance your well-being. You can likewise practice Reiki on others. In fact, you can do anything that your intuition leads you to do.

You simply need to practice what you have learned from this book in order to live a better, happier, and healthier life.

Finally, if you enjoyed this book, please take the time to share your thoughts and post a review on Amazon. I want to reach as many people as I can with this book, and more reviews will help me accomplish that. It'd be greatly appreciated!

Thank you and good luck!

Jason Williams

Made in the USA
Middletown, DE
10 November 2018